Strengthening Programs for Writing Across the Curriculum

Susan H. McLeod, *Editor*
Washington State University

NEW DIRECTIONS FOR TEACHING AND LEARNING
ROBERT E. YOUNG, *Editor-in-Chief*
University of Wisconsin

KENNETH E. EBLE, *Consulting Editor*
University of Utah, Salt Lake City

Number 36, Winter 1988

Paperback sourcebooks in
The Jossey-Bass Higher Education Series

Jossey-Bass Inc., Publishers
San Francisco • London

Susan H. McLeod (ed.).
Strengthening Programs for Writing Across the Curriculum.
New Directions for Teaching and Learning, no. 36.
San Francisco: Jossey-Bass, 1988.

New Directions for Teaching and Learning
Robert E. Young, *Editor-in-Chief*
Kenneth E. Eble, *Consulting Editor*

New Directions for Teaching and Learning is published quarterly
by Jossey-Bass Inc., Publishers, 350 Sansome Street, San Francisco,
California, 94104. Second-class postage rates paid at San Francisco,
California, and at additional mailing offices. POSTMASTER: Send
address changes to *New Directions for Teaching and Learning,*
Jossey-Bass Inc., Publishers, 350 Sansome Street, San Francisco,
California 94104.

Editorial correspondence should be sent to the Editor-in-Chief,
Robert E. Young, Dean, University of Wisconsin Center, Fox Valley,
1478 Midway Rd., Menasha, Wisconsin 54952.

Library of Congress Catalog Card Number LC 87-644763

International Standard Serial Number ISSN 0271-0633

International Standard Book Number ISBN 1-55542-899-1

Cover art by WILLI BAUM

Manufactured in the United States of America. Printed on acid-free paper.

Ordering Information

The paperback sourcebooks listed below are published quarterly and can be ordered either by subscription or single copy.

Subscriptions cost $52.00 per year for institutions, agencies, and libraries. Individuals can subscribe at the special rate of $39.00 per year *if payment is by personal check.* (Note that the full rate of $52.00 applies if payment is by institutional check, even if the subscription is designated for an individual.) Standing orders are accepted.

Single copies are available at $12.95 when payment accompanies order. (California, New Jersey, New York, and Washington, D.C., residents please include appropriate sales tax.) For billed orders, cost per copy is $12.95 plus postage and handling.

Substantial discounts are offered to organizations and individuals wishing to purchase bulk quantities of Jossey-Bass sourcebooks. Please inquire.

Please note that these prices are for the calendar year 1988 and are subject to change without notice. Also, some titles may be out of print and therefore not available for sale.

To ensure correct and prompt delivery, all orders must give either the *name of an individual* or an *official purchase order number.* Please submit your order as follows:

Subscriptions: specify series and year subscription is to begin.
Single Copies: specify sourcebook code (such as, TL1) and first two words of title.

Mail orders for United States and Possessions, Latin America, Canada, Japan, Australia, and New Zealand to:
Jossey-Bass Inc., Publishers
350 Sansome Street
San Francisco, California 94104

Mail orders for all other parts of the world to:
Jossey-Bass Limited
28 Banner Street
London EC1Y 8QE

New Directions for Teaching and Learning Series
Robert E. Young, *Editor-in-Chief*
Kenneth E. Eble, *Consulting Editor*

Contents

Foreword

In the early 1980s, the issues facing writing across the curriculum were those that face any fledgling pedagogical movement: What are its theoretical foundations, how can its techniques be applied in particular disciplines and classes, and what will its future be? These issues were addressed in an earlier sourcebook on writing across the curriculum, *Teaching Writing in All Disciplines* (Griffin, 1982).

The writing across the curriculum movement has now matured. Its programs are organized into a national network, it is discussed in a rapidly expanding literature, and it is even, to the dismay of some, represented by acronyms such as WAC. Thus, the issues its faces are different from those of ten years ago. It is these issues—how to bring about curricular change, how to sustain faculty interest and enthusiasm, how to evaluate established programs, how to collaborate on research with colleagues in other disciplines, and how to continue funding programs—with which this sourcebook deals. Its chapters are written by recognized authorities in the field (three of whom wrote for the earlier collection), people who have earned their credentials by teaching students, training colleagues, and contributing significant research.

This book offers important support for the continued work of writing across the curriculum. Perhaps in six more years, we will see a third sourcebook on this subject. If so, it will surely build on the fine work represented here.

C. W. Griffin

Reference

Griffin, C. W. (ed.). *Teaching Writing in All Disciplines.* New Directions for Teaching and Learning, no. 12. San Francisco: Jossey-Bass, 1982.

C. W. Griffin is professor of English at Virginia Commonwealth University, and has directed a number of writing across the curriculum programs. He has been codirector of the Virginia Writing Project, Capital Site, and codirector of the Virginia Consortium of Faculty Writing Programs.

Editor's Notes

Much has happened in the writing across the curriculum (WAC) movement since the publication of C. W. Griffin's (1982) *Teaching Writing in All Disciplines* just six years ago. A recent survey, the results of which are given in the appendix of this sourcebook, shows that, of those institutions responding, half had brand-new WAC programs and half had programs that had been in existence for three years or more—long enough to be considered "second-stage" programs. Such programs show the continuing success of using writing in all disciplines, but they also mean new challenges for the directors and administrators of these programs.

At the 1987 convention of the Conference on College Composition and Communication, the board of consultants of the National Network of Writing Across the Curriculum Programs held a preconvention workshop to discuss the questions raised by this new stage of the WAC movement. The workshop was oversubscribed, and those who attended found it so useful that the idea for the present volume was born. The chapters that follow, many of them written by members of the board of consultants, deal with the most common problems faced by directors of maturing WAC programs. In the first, I discuss how to translate the enthusiasm generated by faculty workshops into lasting curricular change; the new movement toward general education reform is one place to start. In Chapter Two, Margot Soven continues the discussion of what to do after the first workshop, giving examples of follow-up activities from second-stage programs at various institutions.

The early success of writing across the curriculum at Beaver College has led to many to think of the small, homogeneous liberal arts school as the ideal model for WAC programs. But WAC has become successful at other kinds of institutions as well. Barbara R. Stout and Joyce N. Magnotto, in Chapter Three, discuss the special needs of community colleges and how various programs have been developed to meet those needs, while in Chapter Four Ellen Strenski discusses the challenges and opportunities inherent in WAC programs at research universities. As WAC programs flourish at colleges and universities, the need for articulation with the public schools becomes more apparent; Chapter Five, by Mary A. Barr and Mary K. Healy, discusses the context of WAC

The members of the board of consultants of the National Network of Writing Across the Curriculum Programs are: Mary Barr, Toby Fulwiler, Bernadette Mulholland Glaze, Joyce Magnotto, Susan McLeod, Margot Soven, Keith Tandy, Christopher Thaiss, and Barbara Walvoord.

in the schools, an understanding of which must necessarily precede articulation of programs.

Continuing WAC programs face important questions of funding, research, and evaluation. Many directors of second-stage programs find that outside funding is running out. Programs cannot be run successfully without funding, but, as Keith A. Tandy points out in Chapter Six, it is often possible to redesign a program to run on less. Toby Fulwiler, in Chapter Seven, discusses an issue that arises in most continuing WAC programs—that of evaluating a program's success. In Chapter Eight, Lucille Parkinson McCarthy and Barbara E. Walvoord discuss the unique opportunities available in WAC programs for collaborative research and suggest several models to follow. Finally, Christopher Thaiss, the coordinator of the National Network of Writing Across the Curriculum Programs, ponders the future of the WAC movement. The appendix, based on a survey sent out in 1987–88, is a resource for present and aspiring WAC directors that will allow them to get in touch with programs in their geographical area or with programs at similar institutions.

A closing word is necessary on the collaborative nature of this volume. Those of us represented here have circulated drafts among ourselves, discussed the chapters at several meetings, and shared ideas over the course of several years of professional association. The result is a sourcebook that presents our collective as well as individual knowledge of writing across the curriculum programs.

Susan H. McLeod
Editor

Reference

Griffin, C. W. (ed.). *Teaching Writing in All Disciplines*. New Directions for Teaching and Learning, no. 12. San Francisco: Jossey-Bass, 1982.

Susan H. McLeod is director of Composition at Washington State University, where she initiated the writing across the curriculum program.

The enthusiasm generated by initial writing across the curriculum workshops can be translated into lasting curricular change.

Translating Enthusiasm into Curricular Change

Susan H. McLeod

Directors of writing across the curriculum (WAC) programs are agents of change. The change in faculty attitudes, including the enthusiasm generated by faculty workshops, is a well-documented outcome of such programs (Weiss and Peich, 1980; Fulwiler, 1984; Rose, 1979). But enthusiasm can wane; workshop faculty often move on or retire. How can program directors ensure that the workshops have some lasting effect on the curriculum? This chapter suggests how to translate faculty enthusiasm into curricular change once the workshops are over.

What Kinds of Curricular Change Are Needed?

What kinds of change are we WAC people after? The answer is far-reaching: more required writing classes, more writing required in existing classes. The ultimate goal of all WAC programs is to establish writing as a teaching and learning tool throughout the entire postsecondary curriculum, integrating it completely into every class and every discipline. We are out to change the world. But, while many of us keep this as our ultimate goal, we also recognize that it probably won't happen. The environment of academia has a strong and subtle undertow of resistance to change (Swanson-Owens, 1986), a resistance with many causes. Sometimes entire departments hold out against WAC efforts. I know, for

S. H. McLeod (ed.). *Strengthening Programs for Writing Across the Curriculum.*
New Directions for Teaching and Learning, no. 36. San Francisco: Jossey-Bass, Winter 1988.

example, of a psychology department made up entirely of behaviorists; multiple-choice tests make a good deal of sense in their educational paradigm, while writing-to-learn assignments do not. And there is always a certain group of faculty from all departments whose teaching methods are set in concrete and whom revelation itself would not change. We should acknowledge the fact that some faculty will never agree that writing, like learning, is the province of all disciplines, and concentrate our energies where we know change can take place.

Where, then, should we concentrate on bringing about curricular change? I suggest we look at three specific areas in the curriculum: freshman composition, general education (or "core") courses, and upper-division writing-emphasis courses. All three areas present us with challenges and opportunities for change.

Freshman Composition. The first of these areas is easy to overlook in any WAC effort because it is so close to home. Writing across the curriculum is usually an outreach effort, missionary work in unexplored territory, working with the "other" rather than the "self." But our introductory composition courses are usually the ones we have the most control over and the ones that most (sometimes all) freshmen have to take. Making freshman composition a WAC course means rethinking our assumptions about its content.

Since the days of the Dartmouth Conference, the personal growth model of composition has gained hegemony; students write to know and understand themselves and to make sense of the world around them. I do not want to denigrate this "student-centered" approach, since I believe that the student-centered, rather than the teacher-centered, classroom is an important aspect of the teaching of writing. But the kind of writing assigned in this approach is usually the personal essay, a nineteenth-century belletristic form that requires an introspective writing process, a process much like that of creative writing. Students are expected to look in their hearts and write.

A WAC freshman composition course would include but not give preference to the personal essay and the writing process that goes with it. It would instead view writing as a social process and would include reading selections from all disciplines along with journal assignments where students would react to and make sense of those readings. Along with these writing-to-learn assignments, the course would include the types of writing most commonly required by other disciplines: summaries, critiques, short library research papers, laboratory reports. It would, in sum, become a course in which students come to know not only themselves but also the discourse conventions and expectations of the academic community of which they are now a part. In Elaine Maimon's (1983) phrase, it would introduce students into the ongoing scholarly conversation of the university.

Bringing about this sort of change is challenging because it means that those of us involved in writing programs must learn the critical thinking and problem-solving skills that are involved with these writing tasks. We must work collaboratively with our colleagues in other disciplines in order to learn about their expectations, their discourse communities, their epistemologies. Some work in this area has already been done (Bazerman, 1981; Bizzell, 1982; Bruffee, 1986; Faigley and Hansen, 1985; Jolliffe, 1987), but we need to know more. Bringing about such change is also challenging because we must work within particular departmental and institutional frameworks that determine to a large extent what sort of curricular changes we can make. Enlisting the cooperation of the faculty who teach the composition courses needs to be given careful consideration.

General Education Courses. At many institutions across the country, general education programs are being rethought; the reform is broad enough to make headlines in the *New York Times* ("Changes Sweeping Universities' Curriculums," 1987). Distribution requirements at the lower-division level are changing, interdisciplinary courses are proliferating, old requirements abolished during the 1960s and 1970s are being revived. While the programs coming out of these reforms differ from institution to institution, one idea is common to almost all of the debates: a concern for students' critical thinking and higher-order reasoning skills. Because writing and thinking are so closely linked, it is natural that the place of writing in the general education curriculum should be part of these debates.

Those of us involved in WAC programs should be actively involved in the reform of general education requirements. We need to make sure that what we have learned from the last two decades of research in writing is part of the debate so that the revival of old requirements does not also mean the revival of the term paper as the only student writing assignment. Writing-to-learn assignments (such as the journal or reading log) need to be introduced to faculty involved in general education classes; this is especially important in universities where such classes are very large, since class size is one of the most common reasons faculty give for not including writing. That significant writing can be included in large classes has been proved in a number of institutions; Montana State University (Bean, Drenk, and Lee, 1982) is one example. But there are also successful alternatives to the model of designating certain large lecture classes as general education courses; George Mason University's Plan for Alternative General Education (PAGE) program, for example, offers lower-division students an interdisciplinary option for fulfilling their general education requirements, an option that uses writing to learn in every course (Nelson, 1986).

Upper-Division Writing-Emphasis Courses. These courses are usually an introduction to writing in the professions; students learn the conventions of their chosen discourse communities—how to write like an engineer or historian or literary critic. Because of the need for expert knowledge, these courses are usually taught by someone in the particular field. Many such courses already exist; upper-division writing courses in history departments, for example, are established offerings at many institutions. In some cases, however, these courses now have to be set up, often as a result of a mandate for writing proficiency requirements from some higher authority (a state legislature or a board of regents), as has happened in the state of California. Nervous faculty in various disciplines then find themselves assigned to create a writing-intensive course. Those of us involved in WAC programs need to work with these faculty as they conceptualize the new courses, helping them to look not only at how professionals transmit knowledge in their field but also at how they create that knowledge through writing. Our challenge is to help them create courses that do not simply offer a "forms and formats" approach to writing in the professions but that examine writing and epistemology in each particular disciplinary context and that include writing to learn as part of the theoretical underpinnings. The writing across the curriculum program at California State Polytechnic University in Pomona has been particularly successful in helping faculty design such courses.

How Can We Bring About These Changes?

Before we can change the world, we must study it. WAC directors who want to bring about lasting change in the curriculum should take two steps before setting out to change things. First, they should study carefully the structure of their particular school. Where does the power flow from—that is, who will make sure that changes are implemented? If the school has a strong central administration, then key administrators must be made aware of the need for change in particular areas and must demonstrate administrative support for such changes through commitment of funds, provision of release time for a director of the WAC program, and vocal public support of the move toward change, If, on the other hand, there is a strong tradition of faculty power and governance, arguments and plans for change should be taken to the faculty senate.

Second, WAC directors should establish an informed network of faculty and administrators from all disciplines, people who can sit on key committees and argue for change within their own constituencies. These should be campus leaders and agents of change; because such people are usually among the first to sign up for faculty workshops and seminars, the WAC workshop usually forms the network core. WAC directors should also identify supportive deans and department chairs and get to know them (perhaps by offering a short workshop in a particular department or division); they should attend faculty senate meetings and identify campus leaders who are potential supporters; and they should use formal and informal campus gatherings (such as luncheons, convocations, departmental seminars, and faculty days) to get to know the larger campus community and publicize the WAC program. Follow-up meetings of workshop members, to which other interested faculty and administrators are invited, help to keep the network informed and cohesive; copies of articles on WAC and on curricular change sent to network members also help to keep interest high.

Once WAC directors have determined the structure of their institutions and established a network of like-minded faculty and administrators, they should make sure that network members become members of key institutional committees. Here are some examples of committees that are central to any effort toward curricular change.

The Composition Committee. This kind of committee takes many forms; sometimes it exists within an English department, sometimes it is a campuswide committee, and sometimes it is a subset of a departmental curriculum committee. If at all possible, WAC directors themselves should be on the committee in question in order to have some influence on the content of freshman composition. Due to the lamentable fact that many introductory writing courses are taught by teaching assistants or by temporary faculty assigned to classes at the last minute, these courses tend to be text driven; because of lack of experience or preparation time, teachers often simply follow whatever book has been suggested for the class. It is crucial, then, if one wants to establish a WAC freshman composition course, to recommend or require a text that supports an emphasis on writing across the curriculum. It is becoming easier to find such texts, now that publishing companies have jumped on the WAC bandwagon; on the other hand, one must be cautious, since the WAC label has been pasted on readers that have simply added essays by a scientist or two, just as the "process" tag has been applied to rhetoric texts that have simply added a chapter on revising. Emphases on writing to learn and on the social contexts of writing are the hallmarks of a truly useful WAC text. Faculty involved in choosing composition texts should read Kathleen Welch's (1987) excellent article on the relationship of theory to writing pedagogy in textbook production.

If there is a committee that puts together a common syllabus for composition courses, then the wise WAC director will get on it or will find a network member who can help out; the common syllabus can be a powerful tool for helping instructors hired at the last minute or those new to teaching composition. Course descriptions for college catalogues are periodically updated; WAC directors should see to it that descriptions of the writing program include something about writing across the curriculum.

Finally, if there is some kind of preservice or in-service training for teachers of composition, WAC directors should make sure that information on writing across the curriculum is a part of this training. If there is no such program, it is time to think about setting one up.

The General Education Committee. On those campuses involved with the reform of the general education curriculum, this is an important committee. Alert WAC directors should make sure that several of their campus network members, especially campus leaders who command respect, are on this committee. There is a wealth of articles on how writing has been integrated into general education courses at various institutions; directors should feed this information to their network members on the general education committee, who can use it to keep the committee members informed. Directors should also make a guest appearance at one of the meetings to suggest specific changes. They should be sure to present not only the ideas but also suggestions for implementation, since some faculty are always skeptical about whether integrating writing will really work in *their* classes. It is best to prepare examples of how peer institutions have done it and to suggest that one's own institution can do even better. The goal is to obtain a consensus in this committee that general education courses should have a substantial writing component and that this component should be informed by all we have learned about writing and writing to learn in the past two decades. Assigning more term papers is not the goal here; writing to learn is. There should also be a committee with some capacity to oversee the changes, to certify proposed general education courses, and to monitor the inclusion of writing.

Departmental Committees Across Campus. There are many opportunities for curricular change within particular departments. Departmental curriculum committees are natural places for WAC campus network members; they can keep WAC directors posted as the curriculum is reexamined and can ask for information to distribute to their colleagues. Departmental self-studies and reviews are also good opportunities for network members to discuss the place of writing in the departmental curriculum. Some departments, especially in applied areas, have advisory committees made up of professionals in the field. One can check to see if these advisory groups have made any comments about the writing ability of the department's graduates. I know of a civil engineering department that was terribly chagrined by a letter from the chair of its advisory board lamenting the poor communication skills of the graduates he had hired; faculty embarrassment led to a careful examination of their curriculum and an eagerness to learn about current research in writing so that they could better prepare their students for their profession.

All-University Writing Committees. These committees are usually set up to coordinate various writing efforts across campus and to make sure that proposed curricular changes actually take place. Often these committees are involved with placement or proficiency examinations. Wise WAC directors will work to ensure that these committees do not become punitive in nature, but instead establish positive programs informed by research on writing. It is crucial for committee members to understand the nature of writing development, to see the link between assessment and instruction, and to grasp the fact that, if they are to give us useful information, assessment measures should be direct (a piece of writing) instead of indirect (a grammar test). When discussing assessment with such committees, one should find a resident testing expert and make friendly overtures; such an ally is crucial to one's credibility. Outside consultants, such as Ed White from California State University, San Bernardino, carry even more weight with committees and are well worth inviting for a day on campus. White's (1985) book, *Teaching and Assessing Writing*, should be on the shelf of every WAC director who needs to help a committee deal with the issues of assessment and outcomes measures.

WAC Advisory Committee. If a WAC advisory committee does not exist, WAC directors should set one up and, if possible, chair it. The most powerful and influential people on campus should sit on this committee; they should be given a good deal of power and press but not much work, other than to dispense advice to the chair. The existence of the committee is symbolic, showing that the entire university supports the writing across the curriculum effort, but its presence can also be enormously useful when dealing with timorous departments or faculty. One memorandum to a department chair from a committee composed, in part, of deans from that chair's division can sometimes bring about sudden and wondrous departmental enthusiasm for learning more about writing. Budget problems that get snagged in other committees can be brought to this committee's attention and can often be resolved on the spot. But its most important function is to act in an advisory capacity; WAC directors need the seasoned opinions of some of the wisest people on campus as they move toward change.

Final Thoughts

Some readers may find the suggestions made here a bit Machiavellian. Certainly they are not meant to be suggestions for how one might build a power base within an institution, but rather for how to change the university curriculum for the better. But they are indeed political in one sense: The WAC director needs to be aware of institutional issues that many academics prefer to ignore—issues concerning power and who wields it, turf and who owns it, change and who wants it. We need to be alert and aware, but not coercive; the best change is one that takes place by consensus. By thinking carefully about the issues raised in this chapter and by mapping out a coherent plan of action, WAC directors can help bring about precisely that sort of curricular change.

References

Bazerman, C. "What Written Knowledge Does: Three Examples of Academic Discourse." *Philosophy of the Social Sciences,* 1981, *11,* 361-387.

Bean, J., Drenk, D., and Lee, F. D. "Microtheme Strategies for Developing Cognitive Skills." In C. W. Griffin (ed.), *Teaching Writing in All Disciplines.* New Directions for Teaching and Learning, no. 12. San Francisco: Jossey-Bass, 1982.

Bizzell, P. "College Composition: Initiation into the Academic Discourse Community." *Curriculum Inquiry,* 1982, *12,* 191-207.

Bruffee, K. "Social Construction, Language, and the Authority of Knowledge: A Bibliographic Essay." *College English,* 1986, *48,* 773-790.

"Changes Sweeping Universities' Curriculum." *New York Times,* April 12, 1987, Metropolitan News, p. 1-1.

Faigley, L., and Hansen, K. "Learning to Write in the Social Sciences." *College Composition and Communication,* 1985, *36* (2), 140-149.

Fulwiler, T. "How Well Does Writing Across the Curriculum Work?" *College English,* 1984, *46* (2), 113-125.

Jolliffe, D. "A Social Educator's Guide to Teaching Writing." *Theory and Research in Social Education,* 1987, *15,* 89-104.

Maimon, E. "Maps and Genres: Exploring Connections in the Arts and Sciences." In W. Horner (ed.), *Composition and Literature: Bridging the Gap.* Chicago: University of Chicago Press, 1983.

Nelson, M. "George Mason University Required Writing Program." In P. Connolly and T. Vilardi (eds.), *New Methods in College Writing Programs.* New York: Modern Language Association, 1986.

Rose, M. "When Faculty Talk About Writing." *College English,* 1979, *41,* 272-279.

Swanson-Owens, D. "Identifying Natural Sources of Resistance: A Case Study of Implementing Writing Across the Curriculum." *Research in the Teaching of English,* 1986, *20,* 69-97.

Weiss, R., and Peich, M. "Faculty Attitude Change in a Cross-Disciplinary Writing Workshop." *College Composition and Communication,* 1980, *31,* 33-41.

Welch, K. "Ideology and Freshman Textbook Production: The Place of Theory in Writing Pedagogy." *College Composition and Communication,* 1987, *38,* 269-282.

White, E. M. *Teaching and Assessing Writing: Recent Advances in Understanding, Evaluating, and Improving Student Performance.* San Francisco: Jossey-Bass, 1985.

Susan H. McLeod is director of Composition at Washington State University, where she initiated the writing across the curriculum program. She is also a member of the board of consultants of the National Network of Writing Across the Curriculum Programs.

Since faculty development is the mainstay of a writing across the curriculum program, how do we provide long-term follow-up to the first workshop?

Beyond the First Workshop: What Else Can You Do to Help Faculty?

Margot Soven

Great moments in education are often heralded by significant grants, conferences, or publications. The writing across the curriculum movement is no exception. Most people in the field would agree that Elaine Maimon's six-week faculty seminar funded by the National Endowment for the Humanities in 1977 marked the beginning of writing across the curriculum as a national movement. The Beaver College workshop became the prototype for training faculty to use writing more purposefully in their classes.

Workshops based on the Beaver College model stressed the following principles:

- Writing is a powerful mode of learning
- Writing should be viewed as a process
- Writing assignments should be tailored to course objectives
- Students should write for a variety of purposes and audiences
- Collaboration and peer review should be a part of the writing process.

Perhaps most important of all, the early workshops made the point that we're all in this together. Students must have appropriate writing

S. H. McLeod (ed.). *Strengthening Programs for Writing Across the Curriculum.*
New Directions for Teaching and Learning, no. 36. San Francisco: Jossey-Bass, Winter 1988.

experiences in *all* their classes if they are to become good writers who are able to appreciate the value of writing as an aid to learning.

Early writing-across-the-curriculum pioneers fashioned a package to demonstrate to faculty how these principles could become a reality in their classrooms. Many of our colleagues, eager for alternatives to the drab, if not downright poor, writing they were receiving from students, joined us—perhaps there was something new under the sun! They seemed pleased, excited, even rejuvenated by our workshops, and, thus energized, they returned to their classes to implement the new methodologies.

What has happened since that first outpouring of enthusiasm? The answer to this question is not fully documented, but we do have some clues from our own anecdotal experiences and from studies on the effects of these workshops (see Chapter Seven in this volume). Review of faculty attitudes indicates that, especially during the first years of a WAC program, many instructors do, in fact, implement new assignments and experiment with techniques such as requiring journal writing, giving writing assignments in stages, and conducting peer review sessions.

Now that many WAC programs are ten years old, however, we need to ask if we can sustain these gains in the face of some of the following obstacles: Perhaps student writing hasn't improved as much as we or other faculty might like. Perhaps assignments that have been in use for several semesters have begun to seem less challenging. Perhaps other concerns on campus, such as revising the curriculum, examining accountability and assessment, improving computer literacy, or developing freshman experience programs, now demand more faculty attention. In other words, perhaps "ideas that seemed bright and shiny in the workshop light have dimmed considerably after a year or two . . . due to increased teaching loads, larger classes, administrative responsibilities, lack of collegial support, pressures to research, publish, write grants, and the like" (Fulwiler, 1984, p. 119).

If the grant to Beaver College inaugurated the "first stage" of WAC, Fulwiler's (1984) article, "How Well Does Writing Across the Curriculum Work?," brought it to a close. Fulwiler summed up what he believes are the successes of the eight-year program at Michigan Technological University, but, even more important, he underscored the challenges we all face if we want to keep WAC alive now that the honeymoon is over. He left us with two important questions, both of which WAC directors should ponder carefully: (1) How are we to find enough energy to provide long-term follow-up in WAC programs, and (2) how do we in fact help teachers to translate what happened in the WAC workshop to their own classes on a long-term basis?

Many schools are confronting the challenges of long-term change, and, as Fulwiler points out in Chapter Seven, the number of permutations for accomplishing this change are as numerous as the number of schools with viable, healthy WAC programs. All of them, however, illustrate the following principle: A WAC program must evolve intellectually and programatically if it is to survive. Simply continuing to offer the basic workshop, followed by brown-bag lunches, is not enough.

Many of the WAC programs discussed in this chapter have initiated curriculum change, program evaluation, and collaborative research, but, because these areas are reviewed elsewhere in this volume, I will concentrate here only on the following facets of second-stage WAC programs: new workshops and symposia, collaborative teaching and coauthoring, and opportunities for student involvement. These activities are illustrated by practical examples and by a brief account of how one school, La Salle University, moved from the first to the second stage of its writing across the curriculum program.

Second-Stage Workshops and Symposia

There are many possible formats and topics for second-stage workshops. Some focus on subjects covered in the first workshop, but, in contrast to the basic workshop's discussion of practical teaching strategies, these follow-up workshops are often more theoretically oriented. For example, a first workshop may have concentrated on methods of using writing to enhance thinking skills; the corresponding advanced workshop might explore conflicting conceptions of the meaning of "critical thinking." (This topic is a favorite in second-stage workshops in part because the University of Chicago's very successful series of conferences on writing and higher-order reasoning has had a significant impact on WAC training.) In addition, the advanced workshop often draws extensively for its subject matter on knowledge from many disciplines (such as psychology, sociology, and biology), as well as on theories of rhetoric and composition.

At Spelman College in Atlanta, the ten-year-old WAC program shifted its emphasis to critical thinking two years ago. Since 1986 instructors have been experimenting with special techniques for using writing to stimulate analytical modes of thought. They use standardized learning inventories to evaluate the results. In addition, six instructors have worked intensively with Jacqueline Jones Royster, the WAC coordinator, to develop methods of examining teaching practices. At their summer workshop, entitled "The Teaching and Learning Environment," they describe the results of student inventories as well as analyze their own observations.

The discussion in second-stage workshops typically moves beyond writing to other instructional components, such as lecture style, class discussion, and exams. This happens in a structured way at George Mason University, Virginia, where workshops now cover all language arts skill areas, and at Saint Joseph's University, Philadelphia, where

WAC has evolved into a schoolwide institute on teaching methods and issues. Recently thirty faculty members met for what were billed as two "Bloomsdays" to discuss Allan Bloom's (1987) *The Closing of the American Mind.*

Social constructionist theories of knowledge (popularized in the work of Bruffee [1986], Bartholomae [1985], Bizzell [1978], and others) and their attending pedagogies, such as collaborative learning and taxonomic analysis of discipline-specific writing, are also a popular basis for a deeper understanding of first-workshop topics. Mary Ann Aschaur (personal communication, May 1988) coordinator of the WAC program at Santa Clara University, California, says that "such a theme will tap seminar material—and also consider new applications of it." She adds, commenting on other anticipated benefits of the second workshop, "We suspect that a workshop that builds on the experience of participants, that renews budding alliances and suggests research projects and articles will prove useful and interesting to everyone."

Another example is La Salle University's new workshop "Critical Thinking, Writing, and the Major," which explores the theoretical and practical dimensions of critical thinking common to all disciplines as well as provides a review of discipline-specific modes of inquiry. After examining the professional literature in their fields and their current writing assignments, faculty are introduced to new approaches for designing assignments based on James Kinneavy's (1971) theories of exploratory and argumentative writing.

While most second-stage workshops are designed for an interdisciplinary audience, some are directed at new or special constituencies, such as administrators or individual department faculties. Patricia Bizzell at the College of the Holy Cross, Massachusetts, conducts a series of department workshops on discipline-specific uses of language. Individual departments use what they learn in the workshops to help solve curricular problems. For example, the religion department elected to use journals to help students reflect on personal attitudes that seem to impede learning. The history department uses Bizzell's workshops to clarify the role of the research paper in introductory courses, an issue about which their faculty had disagreed in the past.

Second-stage workshops are also used for training faculty consultants. These workshops can be very nondirective. As Toby Fulwiler (personal communication, May 1988) says, "I open the door and plug in the coffee at the advanced workshop, and the participants take it from there. We critique their presentations and give them tips for shaping their talks for different audiences." At the University of Vermont, faculty from many disciplines who complete the advanced workshop give their own in-house and outside workshops, thereby assuming a leadership role, an important facet of second-stage programs.

Faculty writing workshops, in which faculty either share their current writing in progress or experiment with WAC-recommended writing techniques (such as prewriting, drafting, and revising strategies), are an important component of some WAC programs. A unique variation of the faculty writing workshop is the one at Radford University in Virginia. Faculty who have been granted course reductions to implement new writing assignments come together in groups of four to write about their experiences during a weeklong summer workshop. They write from logs and journals kept during the semester, sharing drafts as they work. Students often join in this process as well. Several essays written during this workshop have been published in professional journals.

In addition to formal workshops, many schools are increasing the number of informal short meetings held during the class day. The purpose of these meetings varies. William Paterson College, New Jersey, schedules three "Writing Roundtables" each semester. These are regular meetings of faculty, administrators, and students "interested in writing, particularly writing generated in the classroom" (Donna Perry, WAC coordinator, personal communication, May 1988). Topics for the spring 1988 series included: "Innovative Assignments That Work," "Collaborative Learning in Action," and "Getting Published: Book Reviews and Fiction."

Elisabeth Latosi-Sawin (personal communication, May 1988) of Missouri Western State College is one of many WAC directors who underscores the importance of using a variety of formats for WAC meetings. She says, "Considerable variety in mode of delivery helps a program maintain interest and model the kind of teaching strategies that will foster critical thinking in the classroom." Her program includes group meetings of faculty experimenting with new writing techniques, panel discussions on such topics as computers and composing, book review sessions (recently, Lev Vygotsky's *Thought and Language,* 1962, and Barbara Walvoord's *Helping Students Write Well,* 1982) and formal faculty debates on such topics as "Is the WAC Movement a Threat to Quality Instruction in the Sciences?"

Collaborative Teaching and Coauthoring

There are many modes of possible collaboration between the English department faculty and faculty in other disciplines. At De Paul University, Illinois, the freshman writing course is linked to a freshman course in world civilizations. Writing topics are related to the civilizations component, and problem-solving strategies introduced in freshman composition are reinforced in the world civilizations course. Each faculty team reports on their collaborative efforts at end-of-semester meetings. These teams have written a textbook, *Rhetoric and Civilization* (Kroker and Fahrenbach, 1988), for the course that combines the history material with chapters on the composing process.

Other examples of coauthoring include *Writing in the Arts and Sciences* and *Readings in the Arts and Sciences,* by Elaine Maimon and several of her colleagues at Beaver College (Maimon and others, 1984a, 1984b) and the *Writer's Guide* (Biddle, 1987), series by Toby Fulwiler and his colleagues at the University of Vermont. In-house publications, often involving many authors, are proliferating and include: *On Writing Well,* William Paterson College; *Write to Learn,* La Salle University; *Improving Student Writing: A Guide for Faculty in All Disciplines,* California State Polytechnic University; *Essays Across the Curriculum,* University of Maine.

Although WAC newsletters are typically edited by the WAC coordinator, faculty from other disciplines often contribute descriptions of their work. These publications, in addition to stimulating faculty exchange, help keep WAC visible on campus. *Literacy Across the Curriculum* (Dawson Community College), *Writ/Talk* (Queensborough Community College), *Writing Across the Curriculum,* (Southern College of Technology), and *Crosscut* (California State University, San Bernardino) are just a few of the many WAC newsletters.

New Roles for Students

Perhaps one of the most powerful ways to sustain a WAC program is to involve students in the teaching process. Programs for writing fellows, modeled on the undergraduate tutoring program developed by Tori Haring-Smith at Brown University, Rhode Island, provide support for faculty implementing new methods of using writing in their classes. Writing fellows—or writing assistants, as they are called at the University of Pennsylvania—are assigned to individual classes to read students' drafts. Besides helping students write better, these programs provide an opportunity for instructors to discuss their writing assignments with an interested student who is studying theories and methods of composition. Instructors may modify an assignment after reviewing it with a writing fellow or may gain new insights into their students' drafts after reviewing the writing fellow's comments. Western Washington University and La Salle University are among those that have incorporated programs for writing fellows into existing WAC programs.

Other Second-Stage Activities

Publicizing the WAC program and the importance of good writing is a meaningful second-stage activity. "Across the University" essay contests help to remind faculty in all disciplines to motivate students to write well. At La Salle, the winners of the essay-writing contest see their work published in an annual booklet entitled *Writing Across All Disciplines: Student Essays;* they also receive a $50 prize. Many schools have developed slick brochures describing both the school's writing program and faculty seminars; good examples are those from the University of Colorado and the University of Massachusetts–Amherst.

Two second-stage programs, one at Pima Community College, Tucson, the other at Western Washington University, deserve special mention for their imaginative approach to second-stage WAC programming. At Pima, instructors collaborate with leaders from business and industry to develop units in writing instruction for all disciplines. The goal is to make students realize the importance of writing in the professional world. Recently a bank president gave a lesson on the connections between writing interpretive papers about Chaucer and interpreting problems in banking. At Western Washington, an interdisciplinary group of faculty grades the junior-level writing test, giving these faculty members an excellent opportunity to exchange views on what constitutes good writing—a discussion that continues after the exam is over, according to Barbara Sylvester, program coordinator.

The La Salle University Program

How does a school know that it's about to enter the second stage of WAC? One sign is the number of faculty who have participated in the basic workshop. By the beginning of 1986, more than 30 percent of La Salle's faculty had completed the summer workshop, and more than half had attended some form of faculty seminar on writing. Another sign is longevity. We knew we had reached middle age when we began to experience the familiar signs of that somewhat unenviable period: an uneasy feeling that we were growing familiar, perhaps even outdated, a sense that it was time to "take stock" and then to take action.

On the plus side, faculty were asking for a new summer workshop. Daylong follow-up seminars with outside speakers were successful but did not meet all the perceived needs. One colleague who had attended one of the first summer workshops asked permission to enroll again; she felt rusty, she said, and needed to "recharge."

La Salle's writing across the curriculum midlife crisis is past, and we have emerged from it unscathed, perhaps better than we ever were. In addition to changes in the program referred to earlier in this chapter, the school has recently approved a writing emphasis course requirement. Summer workshops will be used to train faculty to prepare the new courses. Of course, we continue to offer the basic workshop for new faculty.

Conclusion

There is no reason for writing across the curriculum to disappear; it is not an educational fad. As James Kinneavy (1971) reminds us, since antiquity we have acknowledged the centrality of rhetoric in the university. The writing across the curriculum movement has served to unify the faculty and to focus attention on matters beyond pedagogical practices related to writing, such as what constitutes literacy and what we mean by informed teaching in general. What we do to help faculty "beyond the first workshop" depends not only on our alertness to faculty interest in assigning and responding to student writing but also on our willingness to permit the concept of writing across the curriculum to embrace these broader issues.

References

Bartholomae, D. "Inventing the University." In M. Rose (ed.), *When a Writer Can't Write*. New York: Guilford Press, 1985.

Biddle, A. (ed.). *Writer's Guide*. 4 vols. Lexington, Mass.: Heath, 1987.

Bizzell, P. "The Ethos of Academic Discourse." *College Composition and Communication*, 1978, *29* (2), 351–355.

Bloom, A. *The Closing of the American Mind*. New York: Simon & Schuster, 1987.

Bruffee, K. "Social Construction, Language, and the Authority of Knowledge: A Bibliographical Essay." *College English*, 1986, *48* (8), 773–790.

Fulwiler, T. "How Well Does Writing Across the Curriculum Work?" *College English*, 1984, *46* (2), 113–125.

Kinneavy, J. *A Theory of Discourse*. New York: Norton, 1971.

Kroker, J., and Fahrenbach, W. (eds.). *Rhetoric and Civilization*. 2 vols. Boston: Copley Press, 1988.

Maimon, E., Belcher, G., Hearn, G., Nodine, B., and O'Connor, F. *Readings in the Arts and Sciences*. Boston: Little, Brown, 1984a.

Maimon, E., Belcher, G., Hearn, G., Nodine, B., and O'Connor, F. *Writing in the Arts and Sciences*. Boston: Little, Brown, 1984b.

Vygotsky, L. *Thought and Language*. Cambridge, Mass.: M.I.T. Press, 1962.

Walvoord, B. E. *Helping Students Write Well*. New York: Modern Language Association, 1982.

Margot Soven is associate professor of English, director of the La Salle University Writing Project, the writing fellows program, and codirector of the freshman composition program. She is also a member of the board of consultants of the National Network of Writing Across the Curriculum Programs.

*Survey responses from 401 community colleges show that
many of these two-year, open-admissions institutions have
developed writing across the curriculum programs that
address the special needs of their faculty and students.*

Writing Across
the Curriculum at
Community Colleges

Barbara R. Stout, Joyce N. Magnotto

Community colleges are based on educational and political theories that
suggest that almost all people can learn adult-level material if they are
provided with effective instruction in a supportive environment. Writing
across the curriculum is based on composition theories that suggest that
almost all people can write—and can learn through writing—if they
have opportunities to develop their own writing processes, to write often
in various ways, and to learn the rhetorics of their disciplines.

Because community colleges stand for the broad extension of higher
education and WAC stands for a similar extension of writing, this kind
of college and this pedagogical movement should interact productively,
helping to define and expand each others' purposes and possibilities. To
explore this interaction and to see the present situation of WAC programs
at community colleges, we surveyed 1,270 colleges on the mailing list of

Thanks to Montgomery College vice-presidents Frederick Walsh and Charlene
Nunley and to David Hemenway and Ruth Garies in the Office of Institutional
Research for making possible the survey of American Association of Community
and Junior Colleges members.

S. H. McLeod (ed.). *Strengthening Programs for Writing Across the Curriculum.*
New Directions for Teaching and Learning, no. 36. San Francisco: Jossey-Bass, Winter 1988.

21

the American Association of Community and Junior Colleges (AACJC) by means of a questionnaire administered by Montgomery College's Office of Institutional Research.

We asked about activities, organization, funding, and benefits of WAC programs, and we elicited information about possible impediments to WAC at community colleges. We received 401 responses. In this chapter, we look at what those responses indicate about WAC at community colleges, and we highlight programs that meet the needs of two-year college students and faculty.

An Overview of WAC Programs in Community Colleges

Almost one third of the survey respondents reported that their colleges have WAC programs. This percentage is consistent with other recent estimates of WAC programs at colleges and universities (see the Appendix in this volume and Kinneavy, 1987). Survey responses from 111 community colleges indicated that they are planning or considering writing across the curriculum. The remaining 169 of the 401 responding colleges do not have programs. Eleven reported discontinuing their programs, and one reported reinstating a program after a lapse.

Community college WAC programs vary in longevity, organization, and funding levels. Nine respondents began WAC before 1979; fifty-two began between 1980 and 1984; sixty started between 1985 and 1987. Thirty-four plan to begin in 1988 and 1989.

Some community college WAC programs are organized on a system-wide basis (for example, those in Minnesota and in Arizona's Maricopa district), but most operate at individual colleges. WAC is typically directed by a faculty member, although fifteen survey respondents reported management by an administrator. Multidiscipline WAC committees are common (eighty respondents), as are connections with core curricula or general education (sixty respondents). A few colleges, such as LaGuardia Community College in New York, have language across the curriculum programs, in which writing is important but not primary.

Funding for WAC ranges from the $600,000 in Bush Foundation grants used to establish programs at the eighteen community colleges in the Minnesota system to the annual budgets of $1,000 to $4,000 that are the norm. Compensation for faculty members who direct WAC includes release time, varying from less than one course to full-time reassignment, and, less often, extra pay, ranging from $100 to over $3,000. A few programs have no funding and are fueled by faculty zeal or pushed by an administrator. Fifty percent of respondents with WAC programs identified funding as a concern (see Chapter Six).

The most common faculty development activities are half-day workshops and informal, information-sharing sessions. Full-day workshops, longer institutes, and discipline-focused activities are also popular. The three WAC benefits most frequently cited on the survey are more student writing, increased student learning, and increased faculty interaction.

As this overview indicates, community college WAC programs have much in common with programs at four-year colleges and universities, and this is consistent with their collegiate function (Cohen and Brawer, 1987). Community colleges, however, often differ from senior institutions in curricular dimensions, student characteristics, and faculty circumstances, and many community colleges have developed WAC activities especially suited to their own realities.

The Two-Year Curriculum

Community college curricula are shaped by their two-year status and their "numerous tasks of . . . offering transfer, vocational, technical, adult, and developmental education." (Cohen and Brawer, 1972, p. 7). With varied programs and no upper-division offerings, curricular dimensions at community colleges are more horizontal than vertical, to use James Kinneavy's terms (1983, p. 13). Therefore, some WAC practices that were developed at four-year schools either are not useful at community colleges or must be adapted. Some respondents to our survey identified the two-year curriculum as a problem for WAC on their campuses, expressing a belief that writing-emphasis courses are more appropriate in upper-division programs and voicing a concern about limited time for student growth.

Writing-Emphasis Courses. Obviously, community colleges cannot offer upper-division writing courses such as those at the University of Maryland and the University of Michigan. Several community colleges, however, have developed writing-emphasis courses and subject-composition courses, both of which can accelerate students' growth as writers. In addition, a few colleges have modified the usual two-semester freshman composition sequence.

For example, at Broome Community College in New York, both writing-emphasis (W) courses and a second-year composition course are important components of a newly adopted general education program. To receive the associate's degree, Broome students must take two W courses *after* taking one semester of composition. Then, at the end of their curricula, students must take another semester of composition in which writing assignments are related to their specific fields. In the spring of 1988, Broome offered writing-intensive courses on a trial basis in computer science, mathematics, interior design, chemistry, business, dental hygiene, and nursing. Faculty receive stipends and course-load reductions to develop their W courses; they also attend a seminar directed by WAC coordinators Patricia Durfey and Ann Sova.

Linked Courses. A number of community colleges offer linked or team-taught subject-composition courses to address the two-year curricular limitation. Among these colleges are Richland College and Houston Community College in Texas, Fullerton College in California, Johnson County Community College in Kansas, Bucks County Community College in Pennsylvania, Monroe Community College in New York, and Harford and Prince Georges community colleges in Maryland. At Prince Georges, paired sections of Psychology 101 with English 101 and of History 101 with English 101 are offered. Students enroll in both classes, and assignments in the English composition course are directly connected with the psychology or history course. The instructors each receive three hours of released time during the planning semester to develop their team approach.

The Technical and Vocational Curriculum

Many community college faculty seem to believe that technical and vocational courses are not compatible with writing. In the survey, 154 respondents checked "curricula in which writing is not usually assigned" as an impediment to WAC on their campuses. Again and again, comments such as these appeared: "Community college vocational programs have few academic courses in their curricula and little opportunity for writing in vocational courses," and "WAC seems less adaptable to technologies."

These responses reflect a misunderstanding of major WAC principles, especially the concept of writing as an instrument of learning in any subject. They also indicate the persistence of the assumption that traditional assignments, such as the research paper, are the only way to put writing into a course. In addition, these comments seem to deny the importance of writing in many of the careers for which community college students are being educated.

WAC advocates believe that career courses can (and should) prepare graduates for on-the-job writing. Cosgrove (1986) notes that community college graduates perform a variety of writing tasks and that they find "two-year college courses in their major to be the most helpful to present work-related writing," with "English courses most helpful to academic and domestic writing" (p. iii). WAC programs can serve the technical and vocational curricula integral to community colleges by emphasizing writing to learn and writing that is likely to help graduates become promotable employees.

For example, one of the country's strongest WAC programs deals directly with technical classes. This program, Writing and Reading in the Technologies (WRIT), is at Queensborough Community College (QCC) in New York. WRIT has now expanded into the liberal arts at

QCC, but it began in 1982 in vocational and technical programs. It emphasizes journals and microthemes. WRIT provides faculty with several workshops each year, including some of a second-stage nature that help faculty continue to integrate writing into their classes. WRIT is directed by Linda Stanley, who is supported by an assistant director and department coordinators.

The WAC program at Orange County Community College in New York also functions in technical and occupational courses, with credit-bearing writing modules and writing workshops that are team taught by composition and technical faculty. Writing workshops are piggybacked onto courses in such fields as physical therapy and engineering science. Students take two of these modules to meet a three-credit, cross-disciplinary writing requirement. Christine Godwin is director.

Student Diversity

The open-admissions policies of community colleges affect WAC programs. Around 40 percent of the nation's college students attend two-year institutions ("Targeted Forecast," 1987; Commission on the Future of Community Colleges, 1988), and these students are as diverse as the population of the United States. Some are well-prepared fledgling scholars, equal to their peers at selective universities; others arrive ill prepared for any kind of postsecondary study, academic or technical.

Community college students often take classes part time; some have children; many have jobs. They spend little time on campus and so have few opportunities for collaboration or conversations about their writing assignments. Without juniors, seniors, and graduate students as role models, community college students may not understand the commitment and excitement of serious study, which inevitably includes writing.

While these demographics should not and do not prevent community colleges from having WAC programs, respondents to our survey most frequently identified the following student characteristics as impediments to WAC on their campuses: job and family demands (cited by 44 percent of respondents), wide range of abilities or preparation (42 percent), and little time on campus (37 percent).

The character of the community college student population has at least three implications for writing across the curriculum. First, this variety of students benefits from a variety of writing assignments. WAC directors can inform faculty about the many kinds of assignments that help students to learn course material as well as to become more practiced writers. Second, community colleges need writing centers and other support services for student writers. Third, community colleges with effective—and sensitive—assessment and developmental programs have a better chance of having strong WAC programs.

Support for Student Writers. Writing centers that provide help with assignments in all subjects are particularly useful to community college students. Survey respondents from 136 colleges reported writing centers at their campuses; 78 identified the lack of a writing center as a problem for WAC.

Community colleges often find that their lower-division status provides a staffing problem for writing centers. With no cohort of upper-level students to work as tutors, centers are staffed by faculty, by freshman- or sophomore-level students, occasionally by students from nearby universities, or by community members. Budgeting for faculty tutors and training for student tutors, who are seldom available for many semesters, are regular concerns. To address these problems, community colleges have developed a variety of tutor-training programs and courses. For example, the State University of New York (SUNY) Agricultural and Technical College at Farmingdale offers a special section of English 101 (Composition) as a peer-tutoring course; students who have scored well on the placement exam are invited to enroll, and those who complete the course satisfactorily can become paid tutors, helping fellow students with writing assignments. Ann R. Shapiro developed this community college variation on Brown University's tutor-training course.

Student workshops on such topics as essay exams, lab reports, and research papers are a support service provided at forty-nine colleges responding to our survey. A few WAC programs (twelve respondents) help students through joint efforts with secondary schools. Examples are Brookdale Community College in New Jersey and Queensborough in New York, which have sponsored conferences on writing and learning for secondary school teachers.

Assessment and Developmental Programs. Even the most devoted WAC faculty admit difficulty with students who have severe problems with writing in standard English. Faculty and students alike are more comfortable with writing when students can perform at the level expected in any credit-granting course.

At Miami-Dade Community College in Florida, improved student placement and emphasis on writing work together. Miami-Dade's approach to WAC has been through writing assignments in core curriculum courses. Students are expected to be prepared for writing because the college has strengthened its requirements for assessment, placement, and enrollment in developmental programs.

The connection between developmental courses and writing across the curriculum probably merits more attention. Only 7 percent of survey respondents reported revising developmental courses as a result of WAC. Students in such courses, however, need to practice all kinds of writing, particularly writing that will help them learn the material for all kinds of classes.

Faculty Circumstances

While community college faculty share many characteristics with their four-year and university colleagues, these faculty teach under circumstances that often affect their attitudes toward and participation in WAC.

Teaching loads are heavy at community colleges. The standard assignment each semester for a full-time faculty member is fifteen credit hours, which often means five classes and multiple preparations. An additional class or a few more credits are not unusual. Sometimes classes are large, with thirty or more students to be taught without the help of graduate assistants. Many community college faculty are convinced that they do not have time to assign and respond to student writing. On the survey, 195 respondents (49 percent) checked "heavy teaching loads" as an impediment to WAC on their campuses.

Community college faculty have not been expected to do research (although many do produce fine scholarship). Doctoral degrees and publishing records are not critical to their hiring, promotion, and tenure. This situation provides both positive and negative potential for WAC. The positive is that community college faculty, free from the pressure to publish, may have some energy to devote to student writing. The negative is that many community college faculty are not writers themselves and may not be comfortable dealing with writing in their classes (Obler, 1985). This situation is an interesting inversion of that at research universities. In addition, like their four-year colleagues, community college faculty are specialists who sometimes have problems with "terminology, personality, and turf" (Fulwiler, 1984, p. 114) when writing is encouraged in all curricula.

Our survey shows that several community college WAC programs deal directly with the realities of heavy teaching loads, faculty uncertainty about writing, and specialization by using intensive institutes, one-to-one consultation, discipline-specific activities, and resource materials.

Intensive Faculty Institutes. The Minnesota colleges, Richland College and El Paso County Community College in Texas, and the Maricopa Community College District in Arizona are among those that have been able to provide intensive WAC institutes, which feature composition theory, easy-to-grade assignments, and faculty writing experiences. Richland has annual two-day workshops; El Paso County has a semester-long program with weekly seminars. In the summer of 1987, faculty from all seven Maricopa campuses participated in a two-week session modeled after National Writing Project summer institutes, with stipends and graduate credit. These faculty reviewed scholarship in their fields, both to update themselves and to learn what kinds of writing were being used in their subjects. They also wrote and participated in writing groups, gaining or regaining a feeling for the pain and pleasure of writing, a sensitivity important to using writing well in classes. The Maricopa project is described in "Writing: A Way of Learning" (Bertch, 1987). Julie Bertch is director.

One-to-One Consultations. At North Shore Community College in Massachusetts, WAC committee members have used a one-to-one consulting approach, meeting individually with faculty in various disciplines to help them develop and respond to writing assignments. Marion Bailey is director. Clinton Community College in New York reports a similar approach.

Discipline-Specific Activities. Sixty-two survey respondents said that their WAC programs have included department- or discipline-focused activities. At Montgomery College in Maryland, WAC in its second stage will focus on writing in science, mathematics, and related programs in 1988, on writing in business, management, and related programs in 1989, and on writing in the humanities, the arts, and related programs in 1990. This approach was developed in consultation with faculty in each discipline.

Resource Materials. Books, with copies of assignments from all kinds of courses, can assist faculty in both technical and academic classes; such books are particularly helpful to part-time faculty. Colleges with good resource materials include Quinsigamond (in Massachusetts), Minneapolis Community College, Queensborough, and Miami-Dade.

Other Faculty Support Activities. Some community colleges encourage faculty writing by organizing writing groups and giving luncheons or teas honoring faculty writers. A few colleges give other assistance: Chesapeake College in Maryland provides a writing hot line for faculty and staff; Miami-Dade has used paid, trained "collateral readers" from the community to help in evaluating and grading papers. Orange County's Consultancy Project provides writing consultants for technical departments and for individual faculty who request them.

Support for Part-Time Faculty. In the survey, 101 respondents (25 percent) said that the employment of large numbers of part-time faculty creates a problem for WAC on their campuses. It is often difficult to attract part-time faculty to WAC presentations and workshops; they are often not well paid and usually have other jobs, so they seldom come to the college apart from their teaching times. Helping part-time instructors use writing well in their classes can be an important WAC goal. Distributing resource materials among part-time faculty, scheduling evening and weekend workshops, and assigning full-time faculty mentors are possible methods for improving the situation.

Planning for the Second Stage

Community colleges are moving into the second stage of writing across the curriculum on two levels. Colleges now beginning programs are building on the experiences of those with established programs. Colleges with continuing programs are using the strategies presented throughout this sourcebook as they evaluate what they have accomplished and what they plan for the future. Both groups can take advantage of the natural affinity of WAC with the teaching mission of the community college. WAC programs at community colleges can emphasize writing to learn, writing that prepares students for work or transfer, and writing that enriches students' lives.

Community college WAC programs should be increasingly involved with employers, composition programs (including developmental components), and secondary schools. Faculty and administrators need to know more about the writing demands in the careers for which they train students; only six respondents identified "increased interaction with employers" as a WAC benefit. Composition sequences should be reexamined. Colleges should collaborate with secondary school systems to increase continuity in writing experiences (see Chapter Five).

In the future, community colleges will have a hard time avoiding writing across the curriculum. Not only will transfer students write in upper-division courses, but, because "there is virtually no occupation in our society today that does not require literacy of its employees, . . . the challenge to read and write must permeate the curriculum" (Roueche, Baker, and Roueche, 1987, p. 25). The report of the Commission on the Future of Community Colleges (1988) says that "above all [the colleges] should help students achieve proficiency in written and oral language" in all classes (p. 47). Finally, government agencies are now involved. The Maryland State Board of Community Colleges' recent report *Blueprint for Quality* (Committee on the Future of Maryland Community Colleges, 1986) recommends writing across the curriculum, and Florida has legislated writing into its community colleges' curriculum.

More idealistically, we see writing across the curriculum as demonstrating the "vision and grit" that our community colleges embody (Stimson, 1987, p. 39). WAC is based on visions of learning and literacy, and WAC programs across the country are showing the grit needed to extend higher education to a wider community.

References

Bertch, J. "Writing: A Way of Learning." *Innovation Abstracts* (National Institute for Staff and Organizational Development, University of Texas at Austin), 1987, *9* (15).

Cohen, A. M., and Brawer, F. B. *Confronting Identity: The Community College Instructor.* Englewood Cliffs, N.J.: Prentice-Hall, 1972.

Cohen, A. M., and Brawer, F. B. *The Collegiate Function of Community Colleges: Fostering Higher Learning Through Curriculum and Student Transfer.* San Francisco: Jossey-Bass, 1987.

Commission on the Future of Community Colleges. *Building Communities: A Vision for a New Century.* Washington, D.C.: American Association of Community and Junior Colleges, 1988.

Committee on the Future of Maryland Community Colleges. *Blueprint for Quality.* Annapolis: Maryland State Board of Community Colleges, 1986.

Cosgrove, C. "The Writing of Two-Year College Graduates: An Examination of the Writing Activities of Alumni from Two Western New York Institutions." Unpublished doctoral dissertation, State University of New York, Buffalo, 1986.

Fulwiler, T. "How Well Does Writing Across the Curriculum Work?" *College English,* 1984, *46* (2), 113–125.

Kinneavy, J. L. "Writing Across the Curriculum." In P. Franklin (ed.), *Profession 83.* New York: Modern Language Association, 1983.

Kinneavy, J. L. "Writing Across the Curriculum." In G. Tate (ed.), *Teaching Composition: Twelve Bibliographical Essays.* Fort Worth: Texas Christian University Press, 1987.

Obler, S. "Writing Across the Curriculum Practices of Full-Time Faculty in Selected Community Colleges." Unpublished doctoral dissertation. University of Texas at Austin, 1985.

Roueche, J. E., Baker, G. A., III, and Roueche, S. "Open Door or Revolving Door: Open Access and the Community College." *AACJC Journal,* April/May 1987, pp. 22–26.

Stimson, C. R. "Who's Afraid of Cultural Literacy?" *Community College Humanities Review,* 1987, *8,* 39–46.

"Targeted Forecast: Higher Education Enrollment." *Chronicle of Higher Education,* November 25, 1987, p. A29.

Barbara R. Stout is professor of English and coordinator of writing across the curriculum at Montgomery College, Rockville, Takoma Park, and Germantown, Maryland.

Joyce N. Magnotto is associate professor of English studies and director of writing across the curriculum at Prince Georges Community College, Largo, Maryland; she also serves on the board of consultants of the National Network of Writing Across the Curriculum Programs.

Given the strength of departments, the pressures on faculty to conduct and publish research and to train graduate students in their disciplinary specialties, and the enormous numbers of teaching assistants who are responsible for much of the undergraduate instruction, writing instruction at research universities often seems to be "in spite of the curriculum." Nonetheless, it is possible to run successful WAC programs at such universities.

Writing Across the Curriculum at Research Universities

Ellen Strenski

According to the "Carnegie Foundation's Classification of . . . Higher Education" (1987), 103 research universities, enrolling annually over 2 million students, "offer a full range of baccalaureate programs, are committed to graduate education through the doctorate degree, and give high priority to research" (p. 22). This mission is very different from that of community colleges, liberal arts colleges, or the non-doctorate-granting state universities, many of which were former teacher training schools.

In the narrow sense of training subject specialists to produce better documents (for example, ethnographies, research reports, or case studies), WAC should have strong appeal at research universities. In the more general sense that recognizes the connection among writing, learning, and thinking, however, WAC has come to most research universities only recently, carried on a tide of educational reform to improve lower-division—if not all undergraduate—education. There are, of course, such exceptions as the Prose Improvement Committee at Berkeley, which functioned from 1950 to 1965 (Russell, 1987).

The second stage of WAC at research universities requires faculty and administrators to sort out these different goals and to devise local ways

S. H. McLeod (ed.). *Strengthening Programs for Writing Across the Curriculum.*
New Directions for Teaching and Learning, no. 36. San Francisco: Jossey-Bass, Winter 1988.

for campuses to accommodate them. Whatever else it may mean, WAC means change (Hartzog, 1986; McLeod, 1987). Nonetheless, a residual configuration, unique and constant, of any research university affects the ways WAC is perceived and implemented, and the elements of this configuration include: the power of departments; a "publish or perish" tenure and promotion system that removes many faculty emotionally, if not physically, from the classroom; and an enormous number of graduate-student teaching assistants (TAs) and readers who handle much of the undergraduate instruction apart from lectures. Each of these features creates both obstacles and opportunities for WAC.

Departments

Departments are the research university's "principal organizational component" (Ikenberry and Friedman, 1972, p. 101), and any particular research university is, in essence, "a collection of local chapters of national and international disciplines" (Clark, 1983, p. 31). These chapters (or departments) establish very strong barriers and boundaries across which and within which writing is to occur, and they collectively define what academic writing is through the kinds of texts their members produce.

At the University of California, Los Angeles (UCLA), for example, there are sixty-nine departments of instruction. The distribution of faculty, compared to other kinds of colleges and universities, is disproportionately weighted against the humanities in general and the English department in particular: Of approximately 1,600 regular rank faculty (tenured or tenurable), only 222 are in the humanities. Others are in various other departments and professional schools. Writing instruction at a research university—traditionally, at all colleges and universities, the responsibility of an English department in a division of humanities— must therefore accommodate the needs of students and faculty who have often dramatically different interests and analytical procedures from the small minority in the English department and who write correspondingly different kinds of texts.

Who Should Teach Writing at a Research University? There are three choices of who should teach writing at a university (Kinneavy, 1983; Blair, 1988; Smith, 1988): subject specialists within departments, writing specialists from an English department or a writing program, or a hybrid of the two.

Subject Specialists Within Departments. Specialists, such as kinesiologists, art historians, or physicists, assign writing, when they do so, usually as a bureaucratic convenience—that is, to provide something to measure students' learning and to grade for the course. Composition specialists rightly make much, on the other hand, of the importance of writing to promote learning, not just to measure it. But to promote learning, writing assignments must be carefully designed in the first place and students' papers must be carefully commented on, not just "corrected." Simply requiring students to write about something may or may not prompt learning (Applebee, 1984). Accordingly, subject specialists' assignments, grading practices, and comments on students' papers are often spectacularly ineffective. Moreover, campuses that use this system—for example, the University of Michigan or the University of California, Irvine, through English composition boards that solicit and screen prospective courses in various departments—report that, in the absence of ways to promote and enforce more sophisticated pedagogical awareness, the courses and their instructors qualify for special "writing-intensive" designation solely on the basis of a word count: pages of assigned writing. Training in writing pedagogy is extremely difficult to implement for regular rank faculty who see it tied only very remotely to their professional advancement. Time spent in a workshop on student writing is time spent away from a lab or the library.

What subject specialists can do—uniquely—is recognize and encourage students' struggling, messy attempts as they learn, in discussion or drafts, how to control information with discipline-specific explanatory concepts. Outsiders simply cannot appreciate, for example, what one UCLA sociologist sees and treasures in his students' work as "a creative mess." Moreover, subject specialists have a ready-made forum in their strong departments for addressing WAC. Departmental colloquia are already in place for possible faculty development on topics like "What Is Good Writing in Sociology?" Invited speakers from beyond the department or campus, or a panel of departmental faculty members, can address such questions.

English Department Professors. Writing teachers sent to other departments from the English department or a satellite writing program are unable, beyond a certain point, to guide students in expressing specialized technical ideas in specialized technical documents. Indeed, they can unwittingly give harmful advice. The terms of art in any discipline may sound like jargon and gibberish to an English department instructor who cannot appreciate their connection to tacit explanatory models. For example, the UCLA physics student who wrote "the ball [rolling down an inclined plane] experienced a loss in velocity" was poorly advised to change this claim to "the ball slowed down." That particular physics lab experiment was carefully designed to teach students the law of the conservation of energy, and observing the loss of energy in the ball's velocity to friction was essential to the experiment. Removing the terms removed the physics. This predicament is well documented in "Learning to Write in the Social Sciences" (Faigley and Hansen, 1985).

On the other hand, as British anthropologist Jack Goody (1968) points out, writing is the technology of the intellect. Although English departments certainly don't own writing, by default and lack of interest elsewhere they do currently monopolize the pedagogical tools for coaching the writing process in general and for sensitizing students to the available choices in prose with such discipline-specific explanatory categories of their own as diction, syntax, imagery, voice, and documentation styles.

Team Teaching or Adjunct Courses. A hybrid arrangement has been tried at a few research universities—for example, the University of Washington and the University of California, Santa Barbara (Cullen, 1985)— but it is considerably more expensive. One of the major advantages, however, of providing a paired writing course and a writing instructor is that it automatically provides faculty development, through a personal consultant on how to design better writing assignments that further course objectives, for professors in other departments who generally will not attend workshops.

Where Should WAC Be Housed? The jury is still out on the proper home for a writing across the curriculum program within a university (Blair, 1988; Smith, 1988). One recent study (White, 1987) suggests that "campus leadership and demonstrated expertness in composition" by a strong English department is related more closely to improved student writing than is responsibility diffused through departments (p. 2). But "campus leadership" is predicated on strong institutional support for a vital, well-funded, and conspicuous department or program such as the support for the writing program at Washington State University. Moreover, "demonstrated expertness in composition" requires an unusual— and often expensive—writing faculty, one with an ethnographic interest in the writing done in departments other than English or with professional experience (degrees and qualifications) other than that received by traditionally trained English department professors.

Pressures on Faculty

The professional lives of faculty at a research university are governed by the need to publish their research and by opportunities to augment their incomes, prestige, and influence through off-campus consulting. They are sought out for their specialized knowledge, and they fly around the country, if not the globe, to solve problems. This situation influences WAC in four ways, illuminating one problem, two potential advantages, and one rather subtle and sophisticated implication about epistemology.

The Problem. Many research university faculty find any notion of WAC threatening. They are preoccupied with having enough time for their research and their need to publish it for tenure or promotion and with a corresponding sense of obligation to their subject. Faculty at all colleges and universities may resist "the writing across the core juggernaut" (Labianca and Reeves, 1985, p. 401), but this resistance is especially acute at a research university where the problem of available time is compounded by an epistemology, described later, that values the accumulation and broadcasting of "facts."

Two Advantages. Nevertheless, WAC at a research university can derive advantages from these very features of high faculty productivity and their consulting activities.

High Faculty Productivity. Most research university faculty are very much involved in writing up their own research. Ninety percent of academic journal articles are published by about 10 percent of American academics (Blackburn, 1980), most often in the research universities where "publish or perish" is simply a fact of life. Anyone promoting attention to the writing process in student learning (for instance, recommending the need for instructors to build in preliminary stages for any major writing assignments) can appeal to faculty members' firsthand knowledge of this process and its power for discovery and can point out contradictions in what most faculty expect students to be able to do (for example, generate a thesis and a complete formal outline before doing anything else).

Consulting. The consulting model so familiar to faculty is a ready-made channel of communication between departmental specialists (such as art historians, geographers, and astronomers) who perceive they have a problem (their majors cannot write well) and composition specialists (the expert consultants from the English department or writing program to be called in to solve the problem). Note that consultants are expected to solve a problem and then leave; moreover, consultants are required to solve problems that are defined by others. Departmental specialists worry about the "literacy problem": Their majors cannot write good lab reports, case studies, and so on. They are less likely to be immediately concerned about the connection among writing, learning, and thinking. The slogan "Every teacher a writing teacher" flies right into structural resistance shaped by these consulting practices. The consulting relationship, nonetheless, is a recognizable point of departure for a department or professional school worried about improving students' writing. It means that the university doesn't have to train everyone in composition pedagogy. Instead, specialists at various levels (tutors, teaching assistants, writing fellows, adjunct writing instructors in team-teaching arrangements, and composition instructors in departmentally required writing courses) can be assigned this responsibility.

Epistemology. The pressures on faculty shape a particular epistemology at the research university. Lip service by faculty and administrators to the contrary, this unexamined epistemology is profoundly hostile to WAC promoted as a means of improving student learning. Acknowledging its existence is the first step in countering it and thereby preparing the way for and protecting any fledgling WAC program.

Consider faculty research papers. Value accrues to them from competitive exchange in an academic marketplace through refereed publication and subsequent citation. Writing is a professional life-or-death means of creating valuable intellectual property. It is not surprising that given this reality of their own writing, the faculty at research universities tend to be concerned in their students' writing with quality control, which means "correcting" in order to eliminate error and correspondingly competitive grading.

Faculty writing supposedly captures newly discovered facts, controls them with disciplinary concepts, and delivers them to the public via papers in learned journals. Moreover, because most research reports claim simply to be adding incrementally to our store of data in some kind of disciplinary stockroom, rather than arguing ideas, they can be short. As a result, instructors can feel justified in looking for and rewarding in student papers what one calls "fact density"—evidence of students efficiently packing and repacking the course "content." Seen in this light, multiple-choice tests are a perfectly respectable step away from questions requiring short essay answers.

Finally, faculty research reports like their consulting efforts, claim to be solving problems, everything from AIDS to faulty O-rings in the space shuttle. Indeed, all academic effort and activity by faculty at a research university can be seen as problem solving. It is not therefore surprising that faculty see writing as a student problem (the "literacy problem") that can be solved with the appropriate blend of expert consultation and technology. Moreover, it is not too farfetched to say that faculty view their own courses as attempts to solve the students' ignorance problem. The competitively graded, individualistic products of writing assignments then become for faculty the way students can demonstrate (by displaying selected facts from course content in disciplinary style) that their ignorance problem has been solved. Ultimately, this faculty sense of broadcasting facts creates in turn a mechanical model of students as passive receivers, sitting quietly in large lecture halls. Writing instruction of any kind is seen as a necessarily remedial tune-up so that the student can subsequently better receive and, in turn, retransmit the professor's signals on final exams and papers.

To address this ingrained resistance to a different view and to a broader appreciation of writing is to address the very nature of a research university (Rosenzweig, 1982). But at least isolating and demystifying some of the sources of this resistance may provide help for proponents of WAC.

TAs and Readers

The power of departments and the pressures on faculty may tend to militate against WAC, but the large cadre of TAs and readers creates unique opportunities. Faculty at a research university share responsibilities for undergraduate instruction at a two-to-one ratio with graduate students. For instance, at UCLA there are 3,200 faculty and 1,800 teaching assistants (more TAs than the 1,600 tenure-track faculty). Typically, at a research university a professor lectures (the broadcasting model) to a large body of students, possibly several hundred. Then graduate-student teaching assistants hold small discussion sessions with the professor's students. TAs may assign writing; they usually grade it. If the TAs don't grade student writing, then a reader does, and readers are usually ex-TAs. TAs are crucial in any consideration of WAC at research universities. Their three functions, as John D. W. Andrews (1985) of the University of California, San Diego, identifies them, all relate to writing: "interactive learning, coaching in the higher thinking skills, and providing a communication channel to integrate the course" (p. 49).

Any WAC attempt to help TAs in various departments integrate writing into their instruction encounters the same problems as does that to help faculty: competing time and interests. TAs have their own graduate work (their primary reason for being at the university) to do, and they were selected as graduate students in the first place for their intellectual ability, not their potential teaching effectiveness. Teaching assistantships are financial aid. Yet there's hope: TAs tend to have energy and enthusiasm, and most research universities have at least a minimal TA training program where TAs, unlike professors, can be given explicit instruction.

TA Training in Writing Pedagogy. The training is essential. The most effective training we have found at UCLA involves departmental hands-on workshops that assess assignment design, characteristic student papers, and possible comments for these papers. For example, a typical group of twenty-five kinesiology TAs can examine three or four student midterms or research reports responding to the same topic and representing a range of problems. Grades and comments have been removed. On slips of paper, the TAs anonymously give each midterm a grade; the slips are passed to the front of the room and tallied on the board. Usually there is quite a disparity in the grades, and TAs want to defend their assessments. This discussion leads inevitably to questions about the assignment itself and its objectives and to features of the writing that are either criticized or rewarded as evidence that may or may not be appropriate to the course. Given some consensus on these samples, the TAs can consider and practice possible comments that, in turn, have various objectives— for example, to defend and explain the grade or to help the student prepare for the next writing assignment.

Graduate Writing Instruction. Courses to help graduate students write better themselves are taught at some research universities. More than other aspects of WAC, the existence of such courses seems dependent on the presence within any particular department of a dedicated faculty member willing to incorporate funding for the services of an editor or writing consultant into a grant proposal for a project involving his or her graduate students, or to turn a general-topics seminar into a writing seminar. A good example of the latter is recorded by the distinguished sociologist Howard S. Becker (1983, 1986) of Northwestern University, whose experience teaching freshman English for graduate students resulted in *Writing for Social Scientists.*

Writing instruction for graduate students is a delicate political matter. Graduate deans at prestigious research universities believe that their graduate students do not need writing instruction, and, if they were to need it, then this need should be met automatically by their faculty advisers. A WAC director wishing to set up such a course is best advised to bill it as a course to help graduate students publish their research.

Programs That Work

WAC at research universities is inevitably caught in the middle of conflicting pressures on the curriculum, the faculty, and the students. Issues at stake are political and philosophical as well as pedagogical. Depending on local campus configurations, different players may be in charge of WAC goals: administrators contemplating the establishment of an upper-division writing requirement or an exit writing exam, or the shoring up of general education with more writing instruction; chairs of existing English departments contemplating the establishment of a writing program; faculty committee members investigating the "literacy problem" either in their own department or in the college or on the campus at large. Different WAC arrangements advance different interests; there is no one recipe (McLeod, 1987).

The most promising recent WAC development to emerge at a number of research universities combines the increased attention to general education with the ubiquitous consulting model and with the captive cadre of teaching assistants. Three versions of this combination are illustrated by the University of Pennsylvania's Writing Across the University (WATU) Program, by Brown's Modes of Analysis Courses, and by the Societal Analysis Adjuncts Program at Third College, University of California, San Diego (UCSD).

WATU at the University of Pennsylvania. This program is staffed by TAs from various departments who are trained and advised by director Peshe Kuriloff in conjunction with the Penn Writing Center and the Writing Lab and with faculty from the Graduate School of Education. These TAs, who volunteer for the program and who are paid more for their special assignment and its responsibilities, act as consultants (for example, on designing writing assignments and responding to student papers) to the faculty in various departments who teach the courses to which they are normally assigned. This program is perceived not as a response to a literacy problem but an essential aspect of the university's mission to prepare the trained intellect, in which writing has a valuable place. For a detailed case study, see Hartzog (1986).

Modes of Analysis Courses at Brown University. Surely not coincidentally, Elaine Maimon, who acted as a consultant in establishing Penn's WATU, has, as associate dean of the college, been the prime mover behind Brown's Modes of Analysis Courses. These courses are team taught by a professor and a graduate student, often from different departments or at least representing different fields within the same discipline. For example, one such course, Biology 45 ("Animal Behavior"), combines instructors from behavioral ecology and sociobiology with neuroethology and psychophysics. As at Penn, the purpose is to get students to think better and more comprehensively and to use writing as one means to do so, rather than simply to train narrow specialists to produce discipline-specific documents. Collaborative teaching like this has been a tradition at Brown, and this model of WAC fits it well. For more information, contact Maimon, Brown University, Box 1865, Providence, Rhode Island 02912.

Societal Analysis Adjuncts Program at the University of California, San Diego. Students at UCSD must take, as two of their three required societal analysis courses, ones with writing adjunct sections—that is, special discussion sections led by TAs from the different departments involved in this general education requirement. These writing adjunct sections are enriched with supplementary writing that is assigned, monitored, and read by these TAs. Each writing adjunct section gives six credits, as opposed to four credits for the regular version of the same course; students receive only one grade (not a course grade and a writing grade). Responsibility for training and supervising these TAs is shouldered by Susan Peck MacDonald (1986a, 1986b) who directs the program. For more information, consult her Evaluation Studies numbers 12 and 14, available from the Third College Writing Program, D-009, University of California, San Diego, La Jolla, California 92093.

Conclusion

Proponents of WAC at a research university cannot resolve the institution's structural contradictions and remedy all its attendant educational ills. Consciousness of WAC and programmatic recognition of its importance, however, can help the research university focus on—and mobilize its resources better to address—one of its missions, increasingly urgent and conspicuous: to teach students, especially undergraduates, how to think, how to express their thoughts in writing, and how to communicate them to others.

References

Andrews, J.D.W. (ed.). *Strengthening the Teaching Assistant Faculty.* New Directions for Teaching and Learning, no. 22. San Francisco: Jossey-Bass, 1985.

Applebee, A. N. "Writing and Reasoning." *Review of Educational Research,* 1984, *54* (4), 577-596.

Becker, H. S. "Freshman English for Graduate Students: A Memoir and Two Theories." *The Sociological Quarterly,* 1983, *24,* 575-588.

Becker, H. S. *Writing for Social Scientists: How to Start and Finish Your Thesis, Book, or Article.* Chicago: University of Chicago Press, 1986.

Blackburn, R. T. "Careers for Academics and the Future Production of Knowledge." *Annals of the American Academy of Political and Social Science,* 1980, *448,* 25-35.

Blair, C. P. "Only One of the Voices: Dialogic Writing Across the Curriculum." *College English,* 1988, *50* (4), 383-389.

"Carnegie Foundation's Classification of More than 3,300 Institutions of Higher Education." *Chronicle of Higher Education,* 1987, *33* (43), 22-30.

Clark, B. R. *The Higher Education System.* Berkeley: University of California Press, 1983.

Cullen, R. J. "Writing Across the Curriculum: Adjunct Courses." *ADE Bulletin,* Spring 1985, pp. 15-17.

Faigley, L., and Hansen, K. "Learning to Write in the Social Sciences." *College Composition and Communication,* 1985, *36* (2), 140-149.

Goody, J. (ed.). *Literacy in Traditional Societies.* New York: Cambridge University Press, 1968.

Hartzog, C. P. *Composition and the Academy: A Study of Writing Program Administration.* New York: Modern Language Association, 1986.

Ikenberry, S. O., and Friedman, R. C. *Beyond Academic Departments: The Story of Institutes and Centers.* San Francisco: Jossey-Bass, 1972.

Kinneavy, J. L. "Writing Across the Curriculum." In P. Franklin (ed.), *Profession 83.* New York: Modern Language Association, 1983.

Labianca, D. A., and Reeves, W. J. "Writing Across the Curriculum: The Science Segment." *Journal of Chemical Education,* 1985, *62* (5), 400-402.

MacDonald, S. P. *Third College Societal Analysis Writing Adjuncts Program: An Evaluation of the First Quarter.* Evaluation Studies, no. 12. San Diego: Third College Writing Program, University of California, San Diego, 1986a.

MacDonald, S. P. *Third College Societal Analysis Writing Adjuncts Program: A Report on the First Year, 1985-86.* Evaluation Studies, no. 14. San Diego: Third College Writing Program, University of California, San Diego, 1986b.

McLeod, S. H. "Defining Writing Across the Curriculum." *WPA: Writing Program Administration,* 1987, *11* (1-2), 19-24.

Rosenzweig, R. M. *The Research Universities and Their Patrons.* Berkeley: University of California Press, 1982.

Russell, D. R. "Writing Across the Curriculum and the Communications Movement: Some Lessons from the Past." *College Composition and Communication,* 1987, *38* (2), 184-194.

Smith, L. Z. "Why English Departments Should 'House' Writing Across the Curriculum." *College English,* 1988, *50* (4), 390-395.

White, E. M. "Effective Writing Programs: A Research Perspective." *Crosscut: Writing Across the Disciplines,* 1987, *7* (2), 1-3.

Ellen Strenski is assistant director for upper-division and graduate writing in the UCLA Writing Programs. She is coauthor of The Research Paper Workbook *(2nd ed., 1985),* Making Connections Across the Curriculum *(1986), and* A Guide to Writing Sociology Papers *(1986) and author of* Cross-Disciplinary Conversations about Writing *(1989).*

WAC programs in secondary schools may have been fostered by the same body of knowledge as those in the colleges and universities, but their evolution has been shaped by a different set of circumstances.

School and University Articulation: Different Contexts for Writing Across the Curriculum

Mary A. Barr, Mary K. Healy

Encouraging increased articulation between secondary school and university WAC programs seems particularly useful to us, although we acknowledge the possibility of an "apples and oranges" situation when writing about programs in two such different institutions. The public schools and the universities differ in purpose, organization, and distribution of power. The public schools must attempt to educate all who are eligible; the universities teach only those who choose to attend. Public school teachers are responsible, in their curricular and methodological decisions, to a hierarchy of constituents, including students, administrators, community members, and local, state, and national regulatory agencies; university professors have far greater latitude for curricular and methodological choice and far fewer constraints on their actions.

Institutional differences aside, the role that writing plays in student learning in subjects across the curriculum remains the same. The need for teachers to engage in their own writing to learn is just as crucial at both levels if the syndrome of lecture, assigned paper, and test is to

S. H. McLeod (ed.). *Strengthening Programs for Writing Across the Curriculum.*
New Directions for Teaching and Learning, no. 36. San Francisco: Jossey-Bass, Winter 1988.

change. Clearly, there is much for secondary school and college teachers to learn from each other about the evolution of their respective WAC programs. Articulation between public school and university WAC programs depends, we believe, on mutual knowledge of the context-specific development of each other's programs.

In order that those involved with university WAC programs can understand the developmental context of such programs in the public schools, we will first describe, quite generally, the evolution of WAC programs in the schools. Then we will describe how problems encountered in this first stage have led to the design of second-stage programs.

The First Stage: Raising Awareness

Interest in research on writing development grew in the 1970s in response to a national decline in scores on the multiple-choice tests that purported to measure writing skills achievement. At the same time, an influential study of writing development in British schools by James Britton and his colleagues (1975) investigated students' writing abilities across a range of school subjects. These researchers' recognition that the act of writing is a means of learning in all subject areas received wide dissemination in the U.S. public schools. Individual WAC presentations at local, state, and national conferences for teachers were followed closely by individual school districts offering introductory WAC in-service sessions to their teachers.

In 1980, Arthur Applebee published the first of three studies of writing in secondary schools, which both followed up and expanded on the Britton study. As the Applebee (1980, 1983; Applebee and Langer, 1987) studies appeared, the findings were disseminated via conference presentations, journal articles, and local school district in-service sessions, thus spurring a new wave of interest in WAC.

Generally, the content of these school district WAC programs was essentially informational and did not explore in any depth the theoretical connections between writing and learning articulated by Applebee and by Britton and his colleagues. More specifically, the characteristics of these first-stage in-service programs were: (1) a superficial conception of writing to learn, (2) an insufficient provision for sustained staff development, and (3) isolated individual classroom experimentation.

Superficial Conception of Writing to Learn. Fueled by the public demand for an improvement in "basic skills," state and district administrators and curriculum specialists began to include recommendations for incorporating writing activities into all subject areas in official curriculum guidelines and subject area frameworks.

These recommendations were generally quite vague—exhortations rather than clear rationales or descriptions of specific classroom practices.

Usually the recommendations asked only for the inclusion of the stages of "the writing process" or mentioned generic types of writing—the journal—rather than detailing the purpose and context for these activities and the necessary teacher or peer response essential to promote student involvement and understanding of the subject matter.

A further problem with this first stage of superficial encouragement of WAC was that the resulting student-written products usually did not match the assessment or testing schemes used in the different subject areas. Thus, students who had found journal or speculative writing helpful in exploring their confusion with the subject matter were then evaluated and graded on the basis of a quite different type of assessment—for example, a multiple-choice or short-answer test that required recall of factual material rather than the type of problem solving that their extended writing had encouraged. In many cases, the result of this contradiction in expectations was the students' rejection of the possible benefits of expressive, exploratory writing. Thus, both teachers and students were caught in the bind that results when means and ends contradict each other.

Insufficient Provision for Sustained Staff Development. As already mentioned, in-service sessions at the school and district levels were offered during this first stage to acquaint teachers with the underlying principles of WAC. Often these were one-time awareness sessions taught by visiting college or university professors with little specific knowledge or appreciation of the considerable constraints in the secondary teachers' working conditions. Usually little provision was made for extended follow-up to any of these sessions. Teachers were expected to take the ideas presented, adapt them, and use them in their classes.

Perhaps the most serious disadvantage of these brief awareness sessions was the lack of time devoted to the teachers' own writing about the subject matter of their disciplines. Typically, teachers trained in subjects other than English had little experience with the informal, speculative uses of writing—for example, logs, journals, quickwriting—that are necessary to allow students to reformulate the new information their teachers present. Without such involvement and with the ever-present perceived need to "cover" a set curriculum, most teachers failed to incorporate a range of writing opportunities in their classes after such short-term sessions.

Isolated Individual Experimentation. Another characteristic of the first stage of WAC development was isolated experimentation by individual teachers. Typically, through the institutes of the National Writing Project (NWP) and the subsequent workshops led by NWP teacher-consultants, individual teachers in different subject fields would become intrigued with how writing might aid learning in their classes. They would experiment with and adapt different methods or approaches and perhaps share their results with district teachers at a one-time in-service session.

However encouraging this individual teacher interest was, there was generally little or no district allowance or encouragement for collaboration among subject area teachers who wished to explore different uses of writing in their classes over any extended period. Nor was sufficient additional training or release time provided for teachers to pursue the implications of their experiments in order to restructure the curriculum they felt obligated to cover. Thus, thoughtful teachers reluctantly set aside promising WAC practices either because of lack of administrative support or because of the inexorable demands for covering their set curriculum (Barr, 1983; Healy, 1984).

In summary, this introductory stage of WAC did succeed in establishing the need for the inclusion of writing in the teaching and learning of subjects across the curriculum in the secondary schools, and individual teachers who had successfully incorporated frequent, informal uses of writing in their classes began to write and publish articles describing their classroom successes (Salem, 1982; Wotring and Tierney, 1981). On the other hand, this first stage also revealed a fair degree of disillusionment on the part of administrators in particular, who, after fitting WAC into their already full in-service calendars, discovered that the brief sessions had little real effect. The amount of writing their teachers were including in their subject area lessons did not increase, nor was the purpose of that writing transformed to focus more on the process of learning. Consequently, no link could be made between writing across the disciplines and improving test scores.

The Second Stage: Implementing Programs and Changing School Policies

With the K–12 curriculum reform measures passed in many state legislatures following a bombardment of curriculum reform proposals at the national level, the second WAC stage began. School policy makers, urged to set higher expectations for student writing and thinking, looked to the research in staff development as well as that in language development in order to design new curricula. What they found is the work of Britton (1975), Emig (1983), and Applebee (1980) among others, in which the benefits of writing for clarifying and generating ideas are given equal importance to the use of writing as evidence of what is being learned. Perhaps more significantly, these administrators also found the professional literature equating *effective* staff development with *sustained* staff development.

A recent article synthesizing staff development research in *Educational Leadership* (Showers, Joyce, and Bennett, 1987), for example, speaks directly to school policy makers, those with the budget discretion for staff development. The authors criticize fragmented, skill-based instruction and advocate instead a planned, school-based, faculty-wide, ongoing program. Such staff development involving teachers in all disciplines is in line with the recommendations of some of the influential commissions studying school reform. Generally, the recommendations of these groups call attention to the teacher's own preparation as a key component in the implementation of a more complex curriculum in which students engage in problem solving and higher-order skills. The potentially nurturing context recommended by these groups bodes well for the direction of the WAC movement in public schools.

Currently, the three first-stage characteristics described earlier in this chapter seem to be undergoing a metamorphosis out of which the characteristics of second-stage WAC programs are beginning to emerge:

1. The superficial conception of writing to learn is developing into a deepened awareness of the nature of thinking and learning.
2. The insufficient provision for sustained staff development is transforming into sustained school-based, content-specific staff development.
3. Isolated individual classroom experimentation is being replaced by collaborative learning and teaching.

Deepened Awareness of the Nature of Thinking and Learning. In 1985, a publication (Costa, 1985) by the Association for Supervision and Curriculum Development (ASCD), the largest curriculum study group for school administrators, signaled a widespread recognition that the emphasis on direct teaching of "basic skills" might be depriving students of intellectual stimulation. The publication, entitled *Developing Minds: A Resource Book for Teaching Thinking,* was a collection of disparate notions of what it means to help students think. With an introductory quotation from Walt Disney ("Our greatest national resource is the minds of our children") to set the tone, the collection, although replete with mindless recipes and simplistic checklists for "thinking across the curriculum," nevertheless did propose a national agenda for improving student learning through attention to learning processes. In this proposal, writing became more than a way to test student knowledge of subject matter and use of conventions; instead, it was linked with the students' learning processes and moved to the top of the schools' agenda.

The current test score situation is helping focus school administrators' attention on sustaining support for WAC programs. With few exceptions, achievement scores for poor and ethnic minority students remain low in a context of low scores for the general student population. This situation has become politically unbearable for those who administer schools; test scores are published in the newspapers, schools are compared, and administrators' careers are on the line. The first defense against public attack in the past has been to cite a correlation between race, socioeconomic class, and achievement. Currently, however, models of superior achievement in poor and minority schools, such as that provided by Jaime Escalante and his students at Garfield High School in Los Angeles, discredit the notion of the immutability of achievement by disenfranchised students. Many teachers and administrators are beginning to go beyond superficially conceived programs devoted to "basics" and minimum competencies because the promise of this focus has not been fulfilled.

The latest study of writing by the National Assessment of Educational Progress (Applebee, Langer, and Mullis, 1986) reports as its major conclusion that "students at all grade levels are deficient in higher-order thinking skills" (p. 11). The report goes on to say that "students have difficulty performing adequately on analytic writing tasks, as well as on persuasive tasks that ask them to defend and support their opinions. Some of these problems may reflect a pervasive lack of instructional emphasis on developing higher-order skills in all areas of the curriculum. Because writing and thinking are so deeply intertwined, appropriate writing assignments provide an ideal way to increase students' experiences with such types of writing" (p. 11). Applebee, Langer, and Mullis recommend that *both* reading and writing tasks be integrated into student work throughout the curriculum because of "the relationship between reading proficiency and writing achievement" (p. 12).

New expectations, arising out of similar reports on reading and writing research (Anderson, Hiebert, Scott, and Wilkinson, 1984; Freedman, Dyson, Flower, and Chafe, 1987), insist on a respect for the learner's prior knowledge and the provision for the active construction of new knowledge as well as the comprehension of complex and valued text by all students. Applebee and Langer's (1987) study of writing achievement across the curriculum attests to the fact that writing improves higher-order reasoning abilities. WAC programs are ideally suited to these new expectations for they provide the theoretical base for teachers and the instructional strategies that enable students to reformulate ideas from text.

As a consequence of the new understandings about learning, testing is changing. Commercial test publishers and state testing offices alike are reviewing their tests to align them with the goals of the recent national curriculum reform efforts. Teachers, as well as administrators, are looking for content validity—consistency between what is tested and what is taught—knowing that teachers and schools will be judged solely by the test results. For the first time in U.S. history, test makers are being asked to ensure that their products do not contradict the instructional practices on which WAC depends.

The development of the new California Writing Assessment is one example of a test that supports WAC goals. The test uses a matrix sampling technique that assesses schoolwide achievement rather than individual student performance and therefore does not restrict the curriculum to one or two kinds of writing. Instead, the test evaluates whole pieces of discourse from various genres. Each student writes one type of essay that contributes to the overall school profile of achievement in writing. Selected groups of social science and science teachers as well as English teachers have developed the writing tasks and scoring guides for the assessment to reinforce the necessity of frequent writing across the curriculum with appropriate instruction.

This assessment does more than merely rank students according to their performance. The test evaluates the characteristics that define different kinds of writing, and follows a conclusion reached by Hillocks (1986): "Scales, criteria, and specific questions which students apply to their own or others' writing . . . have a powerful effect on enhancing quality" (p. 249). Using a scoring system perfected by Charles Cooper, University of California, San Diego, and a team of teachers from throughout the state, this assessment gives most weight to the ability of all students to marshal their ideas in a given writing situation. The situations posed represented real tasks confronted by writers of all kinds of writing: autobiography, problem and solution, report, interpretation, and speculation about causes or effects. This new state writing assessment will provide evidence of the development of student reading and writing achievement across a wide range of topics and genres over the years of schooling.

Students cannot succeed on either traditional or new assessments, however, without frequent opportunities to write informally in their classes. By writing their way to understanding, they integrate what they are learning with what they already know. And WAC proponents are not surprised that the quality of student writing improves as students move beyond the formulas and correct answers imposed by those concerned with final products only. This correlation between process and product is central to the nature of second-stage WAC staff development.

Sustained School-Based, Content-Specific Staff Development. Models of staff development have emerged in state and district settings that promise broad dissemination of WAC programs. State departments of education have brought attention to working classroom and school or district models. For instance, Judy Self (1987), a curriculum consultant for the Virginia Department of Education, has edited a collection of articles written by and for Virginia teachers about specific issues in using writing across the curriculum. The collection, *Plain Talk About Learning and Writing Across the Curriculum,* features lively writing by professionals eager to share the results and the solutions to the problems of using writing to learn in their subject areas. The articles are thoughtful, referenced to scholarship in the field, grounded in classroom practice, and mindful of school-based questions. For example, in "When Writing to Learn Didn't Work in Social Studies" (pp. 69–76), Bernadette Glaze, a high school history teacher, explains how she learned to help students put school knowledge into their own words. And, in "Yes, Writing in

Math" (pp. 51–59), Pam Walpole describes the ways her students have used writing to improve their grades and test scores.

In 1985 the California State Department of Education began its subject-specific staff development projects with the California Literature Project, so named to highlight the use of literature as the content of the English class. The project goal was to create a cadre of English language arts teachers, representative of regions and districts across the state, whose task would be to illustrate what happens when a broad-based understanding of language and learning research and the instructional strategies necessary to improve student literacy are implemented. Teaching writing is, of course, one of the most important of these strategies.

Presently, 200 teacher-leaders in the California Literature Project are supported by representatives from district and county offices and colleges and universities to conduct field tests in their own classrooms of research-based methodologies and contents; they also provide services to districts, such as workshops, demonstrations, and consultations, and they conduct summer institutes and two years of follow-up support for other teachers. Teacher leadership in the other academic areas will follow this model of extended staff development, in which writing is incorporated as a fundamental way to acquire meaning from text and experience.

These state models for implementing WAC programs support school staffs who are in the process of developing their own site-based programs—in Virginia, by publicizing the work of individual teachers and schools; in California, by equipping schools and districts throughout the state with informed and experienced teacher-leaders in each subject area.

Aided by the state models that lend credibility and policy assistance, schools and districts in Virginia and California are growing their own consultants. Rather than depending on the traveling expert who cannot help with the specifics of implementation, mature WAC programs now conduct ongoing, school-based staff development with local talent. In the Fairfax County public schools in Virginia, for instance, where Marian Mohr has brought national attention to the importance of classroom-based teacher research, a faculty group at Langston Hughes Intermediate School conducted classroom research studies of the learning being done by minority and underachieving students. As significant as their findings is the district publication of them, entitled *Teacher Research on Student Learning* (Langston Hughes School-Based Collaborative Research Group, 1987), which demonstrates a serious attempt by a school staff to use writing itself to clarify the effects of school goals and practices.

At San Diego High School (SDHS) in California, student writing across the curriculum flourishes, achievement is up by all measures, and there is a waiting list for students to enroll. This scene runs counter to what was happening before SDHS became a magnet school, drawing white students to the inner city. The key to success in this case is the intensive and sustained faculty involvement in WAC staff development. Key teachers like Sharilyn McSwan (English), Beth Schlesinger (math), Norm Leonard (second language), and Stan Murphy (history) work together to design the in-service program supported by a highly trained, full-time in-school resource teacher. Reassigned from her regular classroom, Barbara Storms is this resource teacher who maintains the schoolwide teacher network as well as making connections with district curriculum staff and professional organizations. The program includes full-day departmentwide workshops, a faculty book club, demonstration lessons conducted by a widening circle of key teachers, training for college aids in the writing process, and monthly "writers' forums" to discuss program issues and results.

Collaborative Learning and Teaching. With the understanding that the writing and learning processes require collaboration among writer-learners and their interaction in response to the accumulating meaning on the page or the computer screen, there is a new emphasis on collaborative learning for both students and teachers. The formerly quiet classroom has given way an active, often noisy community of learners. Teachers, supported in this second stage by their administrators who have read that collaborative learning will bring higher test scores, are using response and discussion groups.

The question now is not *whether* to use small groups for response to writing in progress but *how.* Teachers across the disciplines who once refused to include writing activities because they worried about having to grade papers now understand the ways in which collaborative groups can provide response using class- or teacher-made criteria for product evaluation. We do not mean to imply that all teachers can use small groups or that they all understand the value of many readers and writers in the classroom, but these techniques and ideas are widespread, and many local teachers are available as models.

Conclusion

The second stage of WAC clearly depends on this now-critical mass of teachers who themselves use collaborative learning in their own classrooms to create that community of learners so necessary to success in school and college. That these teachers are, at least in some cases, being supported by state and district offices enlarges their scope of influence. And these teachers believe that, just as they must be writers and readers themselves to teach writing and reading effectively, they must also collaborate with each other in order to understand the principles and benefits of collaboration for their students. As Swanson-Owens (1986) points out, resistance to curricular change occurs when the proposed changes contradict what teachers believe about learning and teaching. It should, therefore, come as no surprise when we find that successful WAC programs are found only in those schools where teachers are involved in activities similar to those that they design for their students. More specifically, schools succeed when the emphasis, by both teachers and students, is on writing and thinking about relevant and significant ideas within the subject areas.

References

Anderson, R. C., Hiebert, E. H., Scott, J. A., and Wilkinson, I.A.G. *Becoming a Nation of Readers: The Report of the Commission on Reading.* Washington, D.C.: National Institute of Education, 1984.

Applebee, A. N. *A Study of Writing in the Secondary Schools.* Final report. NIE—G—79—0174. Urbana, Ill.: National Council of Teachers of English, 1980.

Applebee, A. N. *Learning to Write in the Secondary School.* Final report, NIE—G—80—0156. Stanford, Calif.: School of Education, Stanford University, 1983.

Applebee, A. N., and Langer, J. A. *How Writing Shapes Thinking: A Study of Teaching and Learning.* Urbana, Ill.: National Council of Teachers of English, 1987.

Applebee, A. N., Langer, J. A., and Mullis, I. *The Writing Report Card: Writing Achievement in American Schools.* Princeton, N.J.: National Assessment of Educational Progress, Educational Testing Service, 1986.

Barr, M. A. "Language in Learning: From Research into Secondary School Practice." Unpublished doctoral dissertation, New York University, 1983.

Britton, J., Burgess, T., Martin, N., McLeod, A., and Rosen, H. *The Development of Writing Abilities (11–18).* London: Macmillan, 1975.

Costa, A. L. (ed.). *Developing Minds: A Resource Book for Teaching Thinking.* Alexandria, Va.: Association for Supervision and Curriculum Development, 1985.

Emig, J. *The Web of Meaning.* Upper Montclair, N.J.: Boynton/Cook, 1983.

Freedman, S. W., Dyson, A. H., Flower, L., and Chafe, W. *Research in Writing: Past, Present, and Future.* Berkeley: Center for the Study of Writing, University of California, 1987.

Healy, M. K. "Writing in a Science Class: A Case Study of the Connections Between Writing and Learning." Unpublished doctoral dissertation, New York University, 1984.

Hillocks, G., Jr. *Research on Written Composition: New Directions for Teaching.* Urbana, Ill.: ERIC Clearinghouse on Reading and Communication Skills and National Conference on Research in English, 1986.

Langston Hughes School-Based Collaborative Research Group. *Teacher Research on Student Learning: A Compilation of Research Studies Focusing on Minority and Underachieving Students.* Fairfax, Va.: Fairfax County Public Schools, 1987.

Salem, J. "Using Writing in Teaching Mathematics." In M. Barr, P. D'Arcy and M. K. Healy (eds.), *What's Going On? Language/Learning Episodes in British and American Classrooms, Grades 4–13.* Upper Montclair, N.J.: Boynton/Cook, 1982.

Self, J. (ed.). *Plain Talk About Learning and Writing Across the Curriculum.* Richmond: Virginia Department of Education, 1987.

Showers, B., Joyce, B., and Bennett, B. "Synthesis of Research on Staff Development: A Framework for Future Study and a State-of-the-Art Analysis." *Educational Leadership,* 1987, *12*, 77–87.

Swanson-Owens, D. "Identifying Natural Sources of Resistance: A Case Study of Implementing Writing Across the Curriculum." *Research in the Teaching of English*, 1986, *20*, 69-97.

Wotring, A., and Tierney, R. *Two Studies of Writing in High School Science.* Classroom Research Study, no. 5. Berkeley, Calif.: Bay Area Writing Project, 1981.

Mary A. Barr is director of the California Literature Project and is a member of the board of consultants of the National Network of Writing Across the Curriculum Programs.

Mary K. Healy is research and training coordinator for the Puente Project—a writing, counseling, and mentoring program for Mexican-American community college students sponsored by the University of California and the California community colleges. She is also regional director of the International Sites of the National Writing Project and coeditor of the National Council of Teachers of English journal English Education.

*Many established programs in writing across the curriculum
are coming to the end of their outside funding. What are the
options open to leaders of such programs?*

Continuing Funding, Coping with Less

Keith A. Tandy

In well-conceived WAC programs, the ideal situation, obviously, is that
money and other forms of support do *not,* in fact, run out. If we recognize
in the WAC movement not just a goal of improved literacy—or even just
a goal of improved learning through the appropriate use of writing in
all fields—but also a radical challenge to many of the most debilitating
features of academic life as well as a supple and powerful approach to
collaborative staff development among academics, then we know that the
money and support should *not* run out and that the work we have begun
should not end.

But we had better recognize early on that strong traditions and forces
around us are automatically engaged against the longevity of our programs. Among these is the tradition among both academic administrators
and funding agencies of wanting something new roughly every twenty-
four months. Whether or not this is something we inherit from our
frontier history, it is surely a pervasive expectation: In staff development
as in automobiles, Americans want something new every two or three
years. Reinforcing this attitude, in many situations, are the career goals
of those administrators who offer support for our work; a program started
under a former dean doesn't offer much in the way of glamorous résumé
entries for a new dean.

S. H. McLeod (ed.). *Strengthening Programs for Writing Across the Curriculum.*
New Directions for Teaching and Learning, no. 36. San Francisco: Jossey-Bass, Winter 1988.

Because for years, on many campuses it has been the tradition to crank up some new whizbang answer to all problems every two or three years, administrators and funding agencies alike are apt to think of even the most vital WAC program as "something we've already done." Foundations as well as administrators exhibit the infuriating need to own new ideas; a representative of a major foundation once said that he would not provide money for the National Writing Project because "the National Endowment for the Humanities has already done that." The word "done," of course, contradicts our sense of the rhythms, timelines, and depth of the changes we are instigating. We need to be clear on these matters if we are to counter the notion of having "done" WAC. (There are some exceptions to this general rule of foundations funding only ideas that have never been funded before; some private foundations, such as Mellon, Lilly, Ford, and Pew, are still providing funding to start up WAC programs. The federal government is also funding new WAC programs through Title III grants.)

Another problem facing programs supported by "soft" money (grants from private or government agencies) amounts to a kind of paradox: Such agencies almost invariably see their role as providing seed money, not continuous support, yet the institutions usually seek outside funding in the first place because they cannot support grant-worthy programs from their regular sources. The outside agencies hope for a commitment from the institutions they support to absorb successful programs into their ongoing funding. The traditions already cited work against that happening, and so does the fact that, in the case of WAC programs, their energy-intensive nature leads to serious problems of burnout among key leaders.

Finally, administrators may be tempted to see staff development as something that should not *require* support; I was told quite seriously once that faculty are professionals, like doctors, lawyers, and accountants, and that, like those professionals, they should pay for their own professional development. I had to point out that sabbaticals seemed an exception to such a rule, but sabbaticals, this university vice-president thought, were "traditional"; he also did not feel, when I asked, that his own faculty were overpaid, as some of the other professionals he mentioned are.

Working for Continuous Funding

What, in such an unpromising context, can we do? Several things come to mind:

1. From the day support is granted, in whatever form, look ahead and make plans for securing its continuation. If you have not thought that far ahead during all the processes of winning support, the hours you spend celebrating the green light for your program are a good time to start.

2. Analyze your own context and the people in it, including those joining you in leading the program—and do this in writing. Set a calendar for yourself that includes stages of evaluation and reporting, for reports can be a form of educating others both on your blazing successes and on your evolving program needs. Include time in the calendar for program leaders to reflect, assess, and act on the strategies for winning permanent status and full support for the program.

3. Advertise in a decorous, genteel, academic sort of way. We were all taught not to boast, but if you neglect an opportunity to talk to key supporters about your success, you have committed a tiny betrayal of your program. Choose a manner that's comfortable but effective; you should have no trouble expressing genuine excitement and pleasure about the remarkable attitude shifts a specific colleague has undergone, as supported by direct quotes. Some of this is entertaining, but it is functional as well. For example, in Minnesota we treasure the moment when a workshop leader referred to saturation marking as "the 'Conan the Grammarian' approach" to student writing. It's fun to tell this story, *and* telling it chips away at certain Neanderthal attitudes and preconceptions. Suggest to responsible program participants that they address a memo to a key administrator, expressing their gratitude for the opportunity, noting highlights and impressions. This is known as a "win-win" move, one in which everyone comes out ahead.

4. Assess carefully what is essential to your program and what is not, and prepare well in advance to make the case for continuation of the essentials. A year or, better, two years before your program is to end, make a formal presentation to the decision makers on your bottom-line needs for support past the terminal point. Whether you are trying to persuade a foundation to change policy or an administrative group to provide line-item support from campus budgets, you need to know *their* calendar for setting budgets and policies, and you need to make a crisp, clear, and compelling case for continuation.

5. Assume that your claims on resources are only one set among many. This means that you must cultivate "change agents" and others who have influence on your campus. Drinking gallons of coffee in the right locations is one way to learn your way around campus, outside your own department. Consider (very carefully) inviting administrators to attend your program. At Moorhead State University, we were fortunate to have the participation of key people who had great credibility with the faculty; first our president and then our vice-president participated fully in five-day workshops.

6. While you're drinking all that strategic coffee, ask for advice. People love to give it, and often it's useful. Before the Minnesota Writing Project began, a colleague pointed out in casual conversation the problem of absenteeism in workshops, as in conventions, and we worked out a

scheme of prorating stipends on the basis of attendance. That policy produced between 96 and 100 percent attendance in forty-hour workshops, with as many as fifty-seven participants; those are impressive figures for a funding agency to receive.

Semi-Ideal Strategies

Assume that you've had little or no encouragement from the sources of support for your continuing WAC program, yet you are fully convinced of its value and of the continued interest and need of your colleagues. What then? There are ways to "advance to the rear" without actually retreating.

First, there is the goal of seeing writing incorporated in many classrooms across the campus in appropriate and productive forms. Susan McLeod addresses this issue in Chapter One. Any strategy that can produce support for this goal is worth pursuing.

Second, you may have to consider cutting back past the bare bones, the essential core of the program. Having established a precedent of treating faculty like professionals and paying them at least modest stipends for their time, I'm unwilling to revert to volunteer sessions, but a case *can* be made for them. WAC leaders who have established strong credibility with both administrators and colleagues might propose a kind of seminar on classroom uses of writing for interested faculty and arrange for that seminar to be treated as part of the leader's course load. At St. Cloud State University, Minnesota, such seminars, as led by Phil Keith, have had the advantage (compared to summer workshops) of dealing with problems as they come up during the school year. The investment is modest, but the case for such a course assignment still must be made carefully, including evidence that many faculty want to take advantage of the seminar.

Third, the process of refunding a program is likely to be daunting, and the prospects may seem remote. Approaching a new foundation purely for continuation of a program closed out by another agency has little chance of success, so some kind of redesign is advisable. On the other hand, here and there small sources of funding can be found. One ingenious director in our region makes pitches to local "animal clubs"—Moose, Elk, and so on—and picks up $300 to $500 per visit. Newspaper publishers have been approached successfully, with the angle that they have a stake in ensuring that students learn how to write well. Of course, individual efforts to raise funds must be cleared through the campus official(s) in charge of fund raising, or you may find yourself interrupting a long, careful, and major courtship for reasons you know nothing about.

As part of a long-term effort at refunding, you might keep in touch with your original sponsors. In effect, there need be no such thing as a "final" report; as long as you can report on continued activity that grows out of the original investment, those agencies will be pleased to hear of it. Even if doors never reopen, such updates are both professional and courteous.

Much more demanding, but potentially more rewarding, would be a major redesign of what you've been doing. In Chapter Eight, Lucille McCarthy and Barbara Walvoord discuss collaborative research as a kind of second-stage design to supplement a workshop series. My own interest and institutional context are leading me to plan teacher-research seminars. These should be selective, I think, enrolling only those past participants who have been most responsive to WAC workshops, with the expectation of long-term involvement and at least modest but tangible rewards. Such seminars would involve faculty first in studying some of the literature of teacher or action research, in keeping teaching logs on specific courses they regularly teach, and in meeting together to design, implement, and evaluate the use of writing to learn in those courses. As those discussions begin to incorporate general issues of learning theory and discipline-specific teaching methods, I would expect research on new classroom teaching methods to emerge.

What is truly intimidating for the WAC director approaching redesign is not so much the process of gaining support for a different and less-inclusive program, but the kind of careful and collaborative analysis that should precede it. That analysis should take place cooperatively among the program leaders still committed to working with WAC ideas. It should involve a series of brutal writing assignments on which all agree and that address these specific questions.

- What is our core mission?
- What are our resources (in time, energy, and commitment) as a program staff?
- What support can we realistically expect?
- What level of credibility do we enjoy with current administrators?
- What are our liabilities in the preceding areas? (For example, are some staff now committed to new and different tasks?)
- What can we learn from a rigorous and skeptical review of our work to date?
- What does our own pattern of growth as the faculty most centrally involved with WAC ideas suggest about the design of a next stage?
- What are our accomplishments, and are these areas of strength on which we can build a new program?
- What are other recent initiatives in the institution (such as a new core curriculum), and can WAC activities be funded as a part of them?

None of these are quick freewrite topics, but all should be examined carefully by the core leaders before committing themselves to new program shapes.

As if the need for such analysis were not daunting enough, I also anticipate that some program staff may not welcome new directions and that some painful changes in staff may have to take place.

Finally, it may be natural to expect a second stage to start out on the same vigorous, expansive level as the initial stage at its peak. But remember that each year people drown at the beginning of the swimming season because they think they can go as far and as fast as they did at the end of the last summer. A new design will carry with it some of the same obligations to win support, some of the same likelihood of awful mistakes, some of the same difficulty securing enrollment, and so on. Still, while it is true that the workshop experiences we have provided continue to have value, for many WAC programs it is time to look ahead to new designs.

Keith A. Tandy is a professor of English and director of the Prairie Writing Project at Moorhead State University in Moorhead, Minnesota. He is also a member of the board of consultants of the National Network of Writing Across the Curriculum Programs, and was previously coordinating director of the Minnesota Writing Project, a WAC program serving seven Minnesota State University campuses.

The complex and comprehensive nature of writing across the curriculum programs makes them difficult to evaluate. Some measures, however, are easy to collect, and others are worth trying for.

Evaluating Writing Across the Curriculum Programs

Toby Fulwiler

Writing across the curriculum programs have been around for more than a decade—long enough, one would think, to know whether or not they work. However, a thorough review of the professional literature reveals remarkably little evidence one way or the other (1). A limited number of evaluations have been completed that assess the effect of specific strategies commonly associated with such writing programs (2). While numerous books on the assessment of student writing have been published recently, most of their attention is directed at composition activities within English departments and not at the special problems related to writing throughout the curriculum (3). At this time, no comprehensive evaluations of writing across the curriculum programs have been completed, though several books do examine particular components of such programs and provide models that might be useful in evaluating them (4).*

In other words, we don't have as much hard data on the success or failure of WAC programs as we would like—and with good reason. For one thing, these programs are relatively new, most having been established within the past decade, which is not a long time for developing reliable assessment instruments and trying them out. For another, WAC

---

*See Sources and Information on pages 73–74.

S. H. McLeod (ed.). *Strengthening Programs for Writing Across the Curriculum.*
New Directions for Teaching and Learning, no. 36. San Francisco: Jossey-Bass, Winter 1988.

programs by their very nature are extremely complex, multifaceted, and idiosyncratic—characteristics that make evaluation most difficult. There are also more subtle reasons why these programs are difficult to evaluate. In this chapter, I would like to look at some of these reasons and to examine the evaluation procedures most likely to tell us what's really going on in WAC programs.

The Nature of Writing Across the Curriculum

The paragraphs that follow address seven obstacles to evaluating WAC programs that are inherent in the programs themselves.

First, the term "writing across the curriculum" means different things at different institutions. For example, two of the earliest programs from the mid 1970s, those at Michigan Technological University and Beaver College, emphasize different aspects of composition, the Beaver model stressing the differences from discipline to discipline, the Tech model stressing the similarities. Of course, as you might suspect, each model includes elements of the other, and many schools design their programs with idiosyncratic elements all their own. The point is, however, that an evaluation model designed for one may not transfer easily to the other.

Second, writing across the curriculum programs are result oriented, not research oriented, and most of the people who run them are the same. Internal school budgets usually provide money for program operation but seldom for research and evaluation projects. Programs funded on "soft" money are usually required to include an evaluation component, but it is more often a quick and convenient one than a sophisticated and long-term assessment. These evaluations are intended to satisfy the minimal demands of the granting agency—usually, proving that the project was implemented as promised—and not to determine whether or not what was promised actually worked or for how long it will continue to work. Related to this result orientation is the status of program directors: At all but a few institutions, they have been so busy administering and managing that they have had little time for reflection and assessment. Nor have most had any special training as evaluators. The result is that programs are often long on data that are easily collected and anecdotal in nature, but short on either quantitative or qualitative data collected and analyzed methodically or over a long period of time.

Third, WAC programs grow, evolve, and mutate at alarming rates. Once begun, most programs change into something other than what they started out to be. Mutant programs create problems for evaluators who have collected baseline data: When it comes time to evaluate such programs, the evaluators sometimes find themselves comparing apples and oranges. For example, a program that has promised a granting agency that it will improve students' gross writing skills within three years may collect samples of gross student writing from year one to compare with similar samples from year three. However, if, in the midst of this effort, the program begins to stress improved learning instead of improved writing, the initially collected data may be all wrong.

Fourth, the administration of writing across the curriculum programs varies from institution to institution. This means that it is difficult to lock onto a fixed design and study it from institution to institution. True, we may see common elements emerging as typical of WAC programs—collegewide writing assessments, a first-year required writing course, writing-intensive courses, and some form of requirement within the student's major—however, the modes of operating, implementing, funding, and monitoring these several requirements seem to be infinitely varied. Some programs are run by the English departments (University of Chicago), some through writing centers (Rhode Island College), some through interdisciplinary faculty committees (University of Michigan), and some through joint sponsorship by an interdisciplinary committee and either an English department (Georgetown University) or a writing center (Bucknell University). Some programs have provided generous amounts of time for program administrators (Tufts, University of Wisconsin–Stevens Point), some have not. Some have thrived because soft money was available (Beaver and Michigan Tech); some have perished when the soft money ended. Some have been funded centrally through regular institutional budgets (universities of Maine and Vermont), others are part of statewide programs (universities of Minnesota and California), while still others are networked with local secondary schools and community colleges (Loyola in Maryland, William Paterson in New Jersey). In other words, we can identify common practices and program elements and, at the same time, also identify unique administrative and structural differences—making common evaluation studies difficult.

Fifth, measures that are quick and dirty do not seem to prove much. Quantitative measures of either writing or learning ability are difficult to achieve and perhaps marginally useful. The most obvious example is the program that promises an improvement in student writing ability between freshman and senior years, collects and holistically scores hundreds of student papers from each year, then announces that a perceptible difference in writing is noticed from year to year. The casual observer might question whether or not such improvement would be expected with or without a WAC program in place. And, if improvement was clearly evident, could it be attributable only to the WAC program? And, if there was no measurably demonstrable improvement, would we blame the WAC program for adversely affecting student writers? In other words, an evaluation that at first glance seems reasonable represents at second glance a no-win situation.

Sixth, writing across the curriculum programs are amorphous and open ended. Even within well-structured programs, the problems WAC addresses are complex and ill defined: Why do students have difficulty with writing? With learning? With critical reasoning? Is it because they do not know enough? Are not skilled enough? Have not read enough? Have not practiced? Are inexperienced? Can't spell? Aren't motivated? Good answers could include all or none of these, which makes accurate assessment difficult under the best conditions. Comprehensive WAC programs explore all of these possibilities and more with ever larger groups of faculty from disparate departments and disciplines who teach students of different ages and abilities in classes ranging from 12 to 200. It becomes progressively more and more difficult to monitor what goes on in the name of writing across the curriculum as faculty leave workshops and seminars and return to their classes to try things out. The farther away the practitioner gets from the source of his or her training, the harder it is for the evaluator to know what methods the practitioner is actually using. Furthermore, the very nature of the programs is to involve different disciplines and administrative units in one loosely linked structure, making it difficult, if not impossible, for a central intelligence to monitor. Finally, many of the most successful programs promote open-ended rather than fixed-formula pedagogical practice, which again makes efficient, simple data collection and assessment difficult.

Seventh, successful writing across the curriculum programs run deep into the center of the curriculum. In many institutions, so-called WAC programs are more comprehensive than the label alone suggests; they are really language, learning, and teaching programs, involving students and faculty from diverse disciplines. They take place over extended periods of time with sometimes subtle treatments, practice, and activities being the only noticeable changes since the program developed. This may mean that it is as difficult to "prove" that writing across the curriculum works as it is to "prove" that students are liberally educated after four years of undergraduate instruction. Looked at in this way, *evaluating* writing across the curriculum programs may be as complicated as evaluating such things as "good teaching" or "successful learning." What you end up with will depend more on what can be measured than on what is happening.

Measurable Dimensions of WAC Programs

On the other hand, good evaluators, given time, energy, and incentive, can measure anything. That is, we can learn about and measure *some* of what is happening in our programs and report the results to whomever is interested. In this section, I examine the nature and scope of program intentions—a necessary precondition for conducting evaluation studies— and I suggest ways in which the accomplishment of these intentions can be measured.

The writing across the curriculum programs with which I am most familiar are faculty centered. That is, these programs identify the instructors of a given institution as: (1) the primary agents of instruction, creators of both knowledge and attitude toward learning; (2) the determiners of writing assignments, including the nature, purpose, frequency, and kind of writing asked for; (3) the key audience for whom students write those assignments and whose expectations the students must fully understand in order to write successfully; and (4) the respondents and correspondents from whom students hear regarding the quality of the ideas as well as the quality of the language in which those ideas are expressed.

Faculty-centered writing across the curriculum programs generally include some component for training and retraining faculty in designing and responding to writing assignments. And the most common vehicle for such training is the writing workshop offered to groups of interdisciplinary faculty for periods ranging from several hours to several days to several weeks—the intensity varying accordingly. For example, my own university, Vermont, offers two-day workshops for faculty from all disciplines; the faculty sign up on a voluntary basis to attend sessions held off campus in August and January, before classes begin, and in May after exam week. These "introductory" faculty workshops—together with later voluntary "advanced" workshops for veterans—comprise the heart of the Vermont writing across the curriculum program, just as they do for similar programs in all parts of the country.

In looking at the several dimensions of faculty-centered programs, we find a number of places from which to start thinking about evaluation. Where you actually collect data will depend on one of two factors: (1) where you most want to find it and (2) where you think you *can* find it. Let's look at the possible places of emphasis that I've identified:

Community of Scholars. No matter what we once intended in starting a writing across the curriculum program, it soon became obvious as we listened to faculty and read their workshop evaluations that the single most important dimensions of our "Faculty Writing Project" was, in fact, faculty community and collegiality. Of course, it was important that we were getting together to talk about writing, since writing is one of the issues of instruction that cuts comfortably (or not) across all disciplinary lines. But person after person in workshop after workshop stressed simply the value of arranging for faculty to meet someplace off campus with reasonably good food for a couple of days to share ideas about pedagogy, scholarship, students, and the university community in general. (I am not describing exotic settings—rather, the conference rooms and restaurant at the Econo Lodge a mile from campus.) It has become quite clear as I go from campus to campus as a consultant that this collegial dimension dominates most programs that bring faculty together for more than a few hours; in fact, it is an even more powerful experience among those faculties that can afford to spend several days (including an overnight stay) in a retreat-like atmosphere.

While faculty community may be the greatest gain of all for WAC programs, I suspect that few programs put this objective up front when they argued their case before their colleagues, administrators, or a federal granting agency. Yet, if a program is to be honestly evaluated, it must look to measure where the point of greatest impact lies, and if that impact is on faculty community rather than on student writing, it might be a good idea to acknowledge that and collect some data. Many WAC programs could be judged successful simply by the strength of the faculty community they succeed in generating.

What to Measure? If you want to find out how successful your WAC program is as a generator of faculty community, there are some obvious places to collect information. First you collect survey data on who attends workshops, and you keep an up-to-date list of participants. One very simple measure of program success is a growing list of participants who voluntarily attend your program. For example, at Vermont, in the four years from 1984 to 1988, 240 of 650 faculty participated in a total of twelve two-day workshops. These are significant data. Period. In fact, these are the kind of descriptive data that ensure that your thirteenth and fourteenth workshops get to take place.

Second, you ask for an on-the-spot evaluation at the end of every such workshop (and I know some who collect formative evaluations at the end of every day of such a workshop). I ask that they be anonymous five-minute freewrites; I collect these and make sure all of my administrators see all the comments. This is one of the most important measures of program success that I obtain, as the comments are overwhelmingly positive and request continued support for the program. (Quite frankly, many faculty simply cannot believe that the dean is springing for the salad bar!) Testimony about collegiality is strongly embedded in these subjective evaluations, and they are an easy form of assessment to collect, coming as they do from a captive audience. This information, collected at the end of a workshop, is also closest to the direct source of treatment (the workshop) and may, in the end, be the strongest measure you can achieve. Check with participants six months, a year, and two years later by simple mail survey to see how much of the collegial spirit remains. And be prepared for a drop in survey participation corresponding roughly with the length of time away from the program; if you receive better than a 50 percent survey return, you are doing well.

Pedagogy. Most college instructors have had little or no training in how to teach. In fact, many professors actually pride themselves on having taken no education "methods" courses, holding such courses (rightly or wrongly) in low esteem. The result, it seems to me, is that most college teachers teach the way they were taught, relying on the simple dispensation of information rather than on any studied strategies that best exploit how human beings actually learn. In general, college professors take few risks and make few innovations in strategies or techniques—with wonderful exceptions, of course.

Thus, the writing workshops often provide the first actual training in pedagogy for many of the participants. Most of the workshops with which I am familiar are highly experiential and participatory in nature; none of us who lead such workshops would dare lecture (the teacher-centered model) at our peers all day long. Instead, we put them in discussion and exercise situations, often modeling the very techniques most likely to promote more writing in their own classrooms. For example, rather than suggesting that student journals might be a good way for students to explore ideas in a given subject, we provide participants with journals and ask them to write in them often; we write in our own as well, and only later do we actually talk about the technique as it applies to students. Similarly, to discuss how multiple-draft assignments or peer groups work, we ask the faculty to write papers and discuss their several drafts with peer groups. For many college faculty in history, business, biology, and so on, all three of these ideas—journals, multiple drafts, and peer groups—may be new ones.

Looked at this way, the faculty writing workshop is a faculty development project, providing a safe place for instructors in many disciplines to discover possibilities for running their classes differently. In many workshop evaluations, comments on pedagogical inspiration are prominent. These comments are especially likely at institutions that have a large percentage of mid career faculty who, after having taught for twenty or more years, are feeling stale and sometimes burned out.

What to Measure? The first and easiest information with which to assess changes in pedagogy comes from the summary evaluation collected at the end of the actual workshop in an anonymous five-minute freewrite, as already mentioned. Here participants reflect honestly on the immediate impact of the workshop experience, and this is useful information. Remember, however, that, from such information, you will learn only what they *intend* to do once they start teaching again.

In order to find out what effect the workshops are actually having on classroom pedagogy, you will need to survey or interview the faculty at a later date. You can design a simple survey to ask faculty what they are doing now that is different from what they did before they attended your workshop (for a sample of such a survey, see Kalmbach and Gorman, 1986). For best results, send this survey out twice and call each participant if you can. Again, you will probably get your best rate of survey return within the first year of the workshop experience. When you have all the returns you're likely to get, simply tabulate the results and describe what's going on. Sometimes this information can also be obtained by comparing faculty syllabi before and after workshop attendance.

Interviews may be in order if you want more in-depth information about what faculty are doing after having attended a workshop. If you survey your faculty, you can then select people to interview according to their answers; in other words, the answers will tell you who is likely to give you what information. Most faculty will give you an appointment in order to discuss the effect of the workshop. Some, of course, will feel guilty that they've not done enough, but, with the right questions, you can still have a useful conversation.

At California State Polytechnic University in Pomona, for example, Carol Holder interviews each participant in her WAC seminar during the course of the following year, gathering both the new assignments that the faculty member has generated as a result of the seminar and the student responses to the assignments. Such interviews have an effect beyond evaluation, since she is also able to answer questions and help faculty fine-tune their assignments on the spot. Collecting such qualitative data takes quite a bit of time and effort and often requires clerical help; before you commit yourself to interviews, make sure you have the time and the support to do a good job.

Finally, a further check on faculty teaching as influenced by WAC programs might be culled from student evaluations collected at the end of each term at most institutions. Students often mention, even if not specifically asked, the fact that faculty are using journals, peer groups, multiple drafts, and the like. These responses can be compared to those for the same instructor for the term before his or her participation in the workshop.

Improving Student Learning. Many writing across the curriculum programs derive from the work of James Britton and Nancy Martin, at the University of London and from the related ideas of Janet Emig, James Moffett, Ann Berthoff, and Peter Elbow in the United States. They argue collectively that writing ability is intimately involved with thinking and learning ability, and that, in fact, writing will never improve unless learning does. Programs inspired by these thinkers focus more heavily on "writing as a mode of learning" (to steal Emig's phrase) than on writing as a mode of communication. Such programs will be more interested in collecting data that might demonstrate an improvement in student learning ability across the curriculum, rather than an improvement in writing ability.

What to Measure? In programs where learning ability rather than writing ability is emphasized, you will want to demonstrate that, because students are doing *more* writing or *different kinds* of writing, their learning is improving. The "softest" way to find this out, of course, is to ask them. You may find such expressions of faith and accomplishment in student journals, classroom testimony, teacher evaluations, or personal interviews. And, soft though it is, I think such data are important to collect: *Thinking* that something is happening may actually help it to happen; thus, students who believe that writing helps learning are more likely to do more of it and find out that it does help. Simply making students aware that writing and learning are connected may be useful in promoting still more writing on their own. However, such testimony will count little in circles where people expect "proof" that learning has in fact improved.

You might get harder information if you set up limited experimental situations to demonstrate the effect of writing on learning. Here the lines between "evaluation" and "research" begin to blur, but that, of course, simply makes evaluation studies more interesting. One simple design would have populations of similar learners in similar courses compared with each other: Some students would write to learn while others would study in traditional ways, and then they would all take a common examination. You need to know at the outset that such experiments are hard to control; the variations in student abilities and instructor techniques can make the results questionable. If you do not know a lot about such research designs, get help from colleagues in education or the social sciences.

When I conducted one such experiment to examine the effect of journal writing on literature learning, I found that there were no statistically significant differences between the performances of the two groups on a common final exam question. What did this prove? Nothing? Or that journals were as good as the more traditional measures of learning? The preliminary results of other such studies are available for science classes (Wotring and Tierney, 1981) and for mathematics classes (Selfe, Petersen, and Nahrgang, 1986).

It seems clear that evaluation studies measuring the impact of writing on thinking and on learning are just beginning, as more and more faculty and administrators find this aspect of writing across the curriculum to be the most interesting. While many faculty will continue to argue that "teaching writing" is really the business of the English department— or at least of "writing courses"—all will agree that improvements in thinking and learning *are* their business. Evaluation and research studies that could more firmly establish the writing-learning link (or disestablish it, for that matter) will be welcomed by all of us.

Improving Student Writing. Most of the current writing across the curriculum programs began with the intention of addressing problems in student writing and offering solutions that would help students to write better. Those of us whose programs emphasize writing to learn would argue that the only long-term solution to many writing problems—vague theses, unsupported generalizations, weak organization, and the like—is, in fact, to improve student learning along the way. However, most of us would also acknowledge that many aspects of good writing could be taught more directly by focusing on techniques that, once learned, are bound to produce better writing. Such a focus would include: teaching students to determine in advance the purpose of a piece of writing and the audience for whom it is intended; teaching techniques for revising and editing; and teaching faculty how to make more coherent assignments and more helpful responses to students' writing.

In other words, improving student writing is a fairly complex business, involving as it does the students' motivation, knowledge, reasoning skills, grammar, mechanics, creativity, training in a specific discipline, and more. This is why you will find a great number of references to techniques for evaluating written products, some emphasizing particular qualities of a piece of writing (the atomistic approach), others relying on more general impressions (the holistic approach), and still others somewhere in between (such as the primary-trait approach). Which techniques are especially appropriate for use in WAC programs remains an open question.

What to Measure? It is actually quite difficult to prove that students write better because a writing across the curriculum program has been put into place. Sounds silly, doesn't it? Of all the things that these programs are supposed to do, improving student writing is right at the top. But there are good reasons for these difficulties: For one thing, you expect students who attend college to improve their writing from one year to the next no matter what their educational experiences. For another, if students do improve after you've established a program (for example, graduating seniors in 1989 write better, according to whatever measure, than graduating seniors did in 1985), it becomes difficult to demonstrate that it was the program that made the difference and not some other factor (such as different teachers, better secondary preparation, revised freshman curriculum, improved study habits, and so on.) It is also difficult to demonstrate statistically significant differences in the writing abilities of the hundreds or thousands of students in your study unless you collect far more comprehensive data than researchers have collected so far (McCulley and Soper, 1986).

Some things, however, are easier to demonstrate than others. For example, Daly and Miller (1975) have developed an easily exportable "Writing Apprehension Test" to measure the degree of anxiety students have about writing papers in college. This test can be administered in ten minutes at the beginning of a course and ten minutes again at the end; it should pick up positive attitude changes in classes where extensive WAC-related activities have been practiced. I believe that an improvement in attitude is a necessary precondition for any substantial improvement in writing ability.

The most obvious way to demonstrate improvement in student writing will probably be specific to a particular teacher, course, or discipline. In other words, if you want to show the improvement of a limited number of student writers in a particular setting over a fixed period of time, you should have no trouble using one of the several reliable methods of scoring student writing discussed in Cooper and Odell (1977), Cooper (1981), or White (1985), comparing their early writing to their later writing and witnessing some improvement in the bargain. What is considerably more difficult, however, is demonstrating that the reason students write better *overall at your college* is because of the WAC program.

Another approach centering on single classrooms is more descriptive and qualitative in nature: Keep careful records of the writing activities that lead to improvement and show how they are related to WAC. If such classes have used multiple-draft assignments and peer groups in the process of generating papers, then the paper trail will show the degree to which these activities have led to improvement in a particular paper. This approach can be quantified if the instructor is able to say that 80 percent of the papers written using this process have improved—as most second drafts will. This approach can also become comparative if the instructor has sample papers from a previous class that did not use a multiple-draft approach or if other sections of the same class have written similar papers without revision. If you are interested in collecting this kind of information, I suggest you collaborate with a colleague experienced in research and evaluation designs.

Another substantial evaluation project would be a longitudinal study of one or more students over several of their undergraduate years (McCarthy, 1987). Such a study may turn up changes in writing ability, learning ability, and attitude all at once. It will be time consuming, however, and, in the end, it proves nothing of a quantitative nature.

A note of caution is necessary here: We could talk at some length about the variety of techniques for evaluating student writing, but keep in mind that the purpose of this chapter is to look at means of evaluating WAC *programs* and that what you evaluate depends on what you treat. Thus, it is obvious why faculty-centered programs do not readily produce student-centered results: The direct treatment is applied to faculty through intensive workshops; the faculty so treated are expected, in turn, to treat their own students with ideas and strategies learned at the workshop—an indirect treatment difficult to control or monitor. To be safe, measure everything you can, but don't promise to produce positive evaluation results on treatments not under your direct control or supervision.

Improving Faculty Writing. All writing across the curriculum programs of which I am aware began as programs to improve student writing. A significant secondary result in many programs, however, has been the confidence in and knowledge of composing strategies gained by the faculty participants themselves. In the program at the University of Vermont, a significant number of faculty who sign up for WAC training actually do so in order to work on their own writing. Nowhere in our WAC promotion materials is this a stated goal, yet word of mouth about the workshops stresses their experiential nature and the fact that participants do significant amounts of writing while attending the workshops: They keep journals, revise and edit drafts, and receive feedback from colleagues. We do these activities deliberately to put faculty in the role of students and thus generate empathy for the younger writers; we are pleased, however, that the lessons seem to "take" more deeply than that. As one of my historian colleagues, a full professor, told me after a workshop, "I remembered that writing was fun again."

What to Measure? It is difficult to measure whether or not faculty actually improve their writing by attending workshops. If you can afford to interview faculty, collect what they say about the WAC effect on their own professional (or personal) production. A survey by mail is easier and can ask similar questions.

By one means or another, I manage to keep track of the articles, books, and presentations written or given by my colleagues that in any way mention WAC ideas. I also actively promote the writing of books and articles and the giving of presentations that describe the impact of writing on teaching and learning. Through these projects, I am able to argue that WAC programs have a tangible effect on the professional behavior of faculty—in addition to the more obvious social and pedagogical effects. Again, this is not what you set out to do or to measure in the first place, but, once you find it is going on, collect all the data you can.

Observations

The net result of writing across the curriculum programs is both different and greater than expected when the programs began in the mid to late 1970s. Most administrators who oversee complex and necessarily difficult-to-monitor colleges and universities know a good thing when they see it. If you can create a WAC program that produces demonstrable improvements in student writing, you are doing first-rate work. More likely you are directing a program in which significant improvements in student writing—and learning—are taking place, but these improvements are difficult to demonstrate except by anecdote. If that is the case, I suggest you look at everything that is happening at your university (everything within your capability and resources, that is), document it, and see what patterns emerge when you study this information. In active WAC programs with regular points of faculty and student contact, a lot is going on that is making the quality of education better. In the long run, when someone writes the history of this movement, it will probably go down as an undergraduate curricular reform project with noble intentions and unpredictable results. But the more we measure along the way, the more we will, someday, understand exactly what it is that we have created.

Sources and Information

1. A survey of the ERIC documents on evaluating writing programs through 1987 turns up the following:

Roberts, A. R. *College Composition Through an Interdisciplinary Approach.* 1983. 19 pp. (ED 232 523)
A survey of twelve interdisciplinary writing programs revealing their features but not assessing their effectiveness.

Thomas, S., and Keech, C. *Field Studies Report. Evaluation of the Bay Area Writing Project. Technical Report.* New York: Carnegie Corporation, 1979. 35 pp. (ED 191 060)
An assessment of the Bay Area Writing Project.

White, E. M., and Polin, L. G. *Research in Effective Teaching of Writing, Phase I. Final Report.* Vol. 1. Washington, D.C.: National Institute of Education, 1983. 248 pp. (ED 239 292)
A survey of English department writing programs at nineteen California state universities.

2. Among the studies that evaluate program components within larger WAC projects are the following:

Wotring, A., and Tierney, R. *Two Studies of Writing in High School Science.* Classroom Research Study, no. 5. Berkeley, Calif.: Bay Area Writing Project, 1981.

Young, A., and Fulwiler, T. (eds.). *Writing Across the Disciplines: Research into Practice.* Upper Montclair, N.J.: Boynton/Cook, 1986.

3. The following books describe processes suitable for evaluating composition courses and writing programs in general:

Cooper, C. R. (ed.). *The Nature and Measurement of Competency in English.* Urbana, Ill.: National Council of Teachers of English, 1981.

Cooper, C. R., and Odell, L. (eds.). *Evaluating Writing.* Urbana, Ill.: National Council of Teachers of English, 1977.

Faigley, L., Cherry, R., Jolliffe, D., and Skinner, A. *Assessing Writers' Knowledge and Processes of Composing.* Norwood, N.J.: Ablex, 1985.

Faigley, L., and Witte, S. P. *Evaluating College Writing Programs.* Carbondale: Southern Illinois University Press, 1984.

Greenberg, K., Wiener, H., and Donovan, R. *Writing Assessment: Issues and Strategies.* New York: Longman, 1986.

Hartzog, C. P. *Composition and the Academy: A Study of Writing Program Administration.* New York: Modern Language Association, 1986.

Hillocks, G., Jr. *Research on Written Composition: New Directions for Teaching.* Urbana, Ill.: ERIC Clearinghouse on Reading and Communication Skills and National Conference on Research in English, 1986.

White, E. M. *Teaching and Assessing Writing: Recent Advances in Understanding, Evaluating, and Improving Student Performance.* San Francisco: Jossey-Bass, 1985.

(Additional information on writing program evaluation is found regularly in the periodical *Writing Program Administration [WPA]* published by the Council of Writing Program Administrators.)

4. The following books anecdotally describe successful WAC practices within classroom settings by teachers across the curriculum:

Fulwiler, T. (ed.). *The Journal Book.* Portsmouth, N.H.: Heinemann, 1987.

Gere, A. (ed.). *Roots in the Sawdust.* Urbana, Ill.: National Council of Teachers of English, 1985.

Thaiss, C. (ed.). *Writing to Learn.* Dubuque, Iowa: Kendall-Hunt, 1981.

The following books describe processes aimed particularly at evaluating programs in writing across the curriculum:

Davis, B. G., Scriven, M., and Thomas, S. *The Evaluation of Composition Instruction.* (2nd ed.) New York: Teachers College Press, 1988.

Young, A., and Fulwiler, T. (eds.). *Writing Across the Disciplines: Research into Practice.* Upper Montclair, N.J.: Boynton/Cook, 1986.

References

Cooper, C. R. *The Nature and Measurement of Competency in English.* Urbana, Ill.: National Council of Teachers of English, 1981.
Cooper, C. R., and Odell, L. (eds.). *Evaluating Writing.* Urbana, Ill.: National Council of Teachers of English, 1977.

Daly, J., and Miller, M. D. "The Empirical Development of an Instrument to Measure Writing Apprehension." *Research in the Teaching of English*, 1975, *9*, 242–249.

Kalmbach, J., and Gorman, M. E. "Surveying Classroom Practices." In A. Young and T. Fulwiler (eds.), *Writing Across the Disciplines: Research into Practice.* Upper Montclair, N.J.: Boynton/Cook, 1986.

McCarthy, L. P. "A Stranger in Strange Lands: A College Student Writing Across the Curriculum." *Research in the Teaching of English*, 1987, *21* (3), 233–265.

McCulley, G., and Soper, J. "Assessing the Writing Skills of Engineering Students." In A. Young and T. Fulwiler (eds.), *Writing Across the Disciplines: Research into Practice.* Upper Montclair, N.J.: Boynton/Cook, 1986.

Selfe, C., Petersen, B., and Nahrgang, C. "Journal Writing in Mathematics." In A. Young and T. Fulwiler (eds.), *Writing Across the Disciplines: Research into Practice.* Upper Montclair, N.J.: Boynton/Cook, 1986.

White, E. M. *Teaching and Assessing Writing: Recent Advances in Understanding, Evaluating, and Improving Student Performance.* San Francisco: Jossey-Bass, 1985.

Wotring, A., and Tierney, R. *Two Studies of Writing in High School Science.* Classroom Research Study, no. 5. Berkeley, Calif.: Bay Area Writing Project, 1981.

Toby Fulwiler directs the writing program at the University of Vermont and is a member of the board of consultants of the National Network of Writing Across the Curriculum Programs.

In collaborative research projects, teachers from two or more disciplines work together in order to understand better their students' thinking and writing.

Models for Collaborative Research in Writing Across the Curriculum

Lucille Parkinson McCarthy, Barbara E. Walvoord

> *The continuing surface of educational problems requires an atmosphere in which sharing on how to build collaborative strategies is considered as valuable as dissemination of research results.*
> *Wallat, Green, Conlin, and Haramis (1981, p. 110)*

In this chapter we will argue that collaborative research in writing across the curriculum is a powerful companion to the usual workshop activities of listening, reading, and discussing. In WAC workshops, we have offered our colleagues in the disciplines a theoretical framework for understanding writing, and we have made general suggestions about pedagogy. We have been gratified by the response: Many of our colleagues have incorporated into their teaching a concern for the writing process, the view that writing is a mode of learning, and such strategies as journals, invention and revision activities, and peer response groups. In response to writing across the curriculum workshops, teachers from a variety of disciplines have reevaluated their assumptions about writing and learning, and they have experimented with changes in their classrooms.

S. H. McLeod (ed.). *Strengthening Programs for Writing Across the Curriculum.*
New Directions for Teaching and Learning, no. 36. San Francisco: Jossey-Bass, Winter 1988.

The theoretical and pedagogical direction given in workshops, however, is a general one. Of necessity it is based on the published literature, which consists in large part of studies of K–12 students or college composition students, often in small numbers and often in experimental rather than natural settings. There is little in WAC workshops that can specifically tell a college biology teacher, for example, how her or his students are thinking as they write for a particular assignment, nor can workshops tell instructors what problems their students are having or how some students go about solving these problems while others do not. The only way instructors can know how their students are thinking and the only way they can understand how their newly learned teaching strategies influence that thinking is through close observation of their students. Systematic investigation in their own (and others') classrooms is, we feel, a central component of writing across the curriculum's "second stage." It is through such investigation that teachers will continue to grow after the workshops are finished.

The three models or structures that we describe for writing across the curriculum research are all collaborative. They are drawn from our own experiences in ten collaborations and those of some twenty other pairs or groups of teacher-researchers who have studied or are presently studying writing, thinking, and learning in various academic contexts. In each of these approximately thirty collaborations, teacher-researchers from two or more disciplines have worked together to shape their research questions and design systematic data collection and analysis procedures. And they have, in some cases, coauthored reports of their research to share with their colleagues in one or more disciplines. The three models we present here reflect the structural arrangements of the collaborations. These structures do not, however, determine the research methods that the collaborators chose. Within each of the three models, researchers have drawn on various research traditions, both experimental and naturalistic, for their theoretical assumptions, research methods, and ways of assessing reliability and validity. All thirty projects, however, explore the questions that lie at the heart of the writing across the curriculum endeavor:

- What constitutes "good" writing in various disciplines, and what are the learning and writing tasks that students must master in each? Which textual features and learning and writing tasks are discipline-specific, and which are general?
- How do students interpret these tasks, and how do they go about producing "good" writing in each discipline and classroom?
- What can we do to help students in this process?

These questions are best answered collaboratively. Underlying much writing across the curriculum research is the assumption, summarized so lucidly by Bruffee (1984), that knowledge both comes from and results in social interaction. We need help if we are to understand the social and intellectual dynamics within our own disciplines and classrooms, dynamics that are so familiar that they may be largely invisible to us. As one teacher-researcher put it, "It's immensely illuminating to see your students and their writing through someone else's eyes. After seventeen years of working alone, I'd developed a kind of tunnel vision." And we need help to understand, and eventually to *perceive*, through the frameworks of others. In writing across the curriculum research, constructing knowledge in interaction is both the central activity of the research process and, at the same time, the object of research. We work together to discover how knowledge is generated in spoken and written interaction in various disciplines and classrooms. And then we ask how we can help students negotiate entry into the "conversations" in those communities, and how, once they are in such communities, we may best support their growth and development there.

Models for Collaborative Research Projects

The story of each of the thirty collaborations we examined was unique. The projects' beginnings and specific goals were different, as were their evolutions, their satisfactions and frustrations, and their outcomes. In our conversations with researchers as we prepared this chapter, we heard about "arguments," "clashes," "furious debates," and "fierce discussions." We also heard about "compromise," "consensus," and "working, tugging, pulling." One researcher told us that her project had been "filled with nightmares," whereas the next one we spoke with said that his project had been "fun, a wonderful alternative to the monastic loneliness of academic writing."

Frequently surfacing in researchers' talk was the comparison between collaboration and marriage. One woman, a writing specialist, spoke of "proposing" to a colleague in the business school and of drawing up a sort of "prenuptial agreement" before undertaking the collaboration. In their agreement they defined their goals for the project and their individual and joint responsibilities, made time commitments, and agreed on such manuscript management issues as who would be first author on their coauthored work. (Hers would be first in writing journals, his in business.) Another writing specialist spoke of the successful "matchmaking" that had paired her with her psychologist collaborator and about how their collaboration had become richer over time as they came to trust each other more. Her psychologist partner told us, "It was a beautiful marriage. We had complementary skills and strengths and resources. Neither of us could have done it alone." Another writing specialist said that negotiating role and power relationships is as "tricky" between research collaborators as it is between newlyweds. He said that he wasn't exactly sure how "compatibility" was achieved in either case, but "it's got something to do with choosing each other, with being equally strongly motivated, and with learning eventually to speak the same language." We also heard about a project where there were "irreconcilable differences" and eventual "divorce." This marriage metaphor suggests just how close and intense these collaborative relationships are.

Although the stories of the collaborations are unique, similarities do exist in their structural arrangements. In this chapter we will define three structural models and describe an example of each, paying special attention in our examples to qualities that appear to characterize many successful collaborations. Finally, we will recommend several sources of information about research methodology.

As we chose the collaborative projects to use as examples in this chapter, we were guided by three criteria. First, the project must have resulted in some sort of publication. Second, it must have been a satisfying experience for the researchers. And, finally, it had to be a collaboration about which we could obtain abundant information. This last criteria was, of course, best fulfilled by projects we had been acquainted with for an extended period of time. Because three of the five projects we describe here were carried out by members of our own community, the Maryland Writing Project, we knew them particularly well. Our five example projects are, however, typical in many ways of the thirty we examined. Our aim in this chapter is to offer ideas and guidance to those who are beginning systematic classroom research, an activity we consider central to writing across the curriculum's second stage. (For a description of the Maryland Writing Project and the Baltimore Area Consortium for Writing Across the Curriculum, see Walvoord and Dowling, in press.)

Collaborative Research Model 1: The Focused Pair. In this model, which is the most common, a writing specialist pairs with a teacher from another discipline, and together they study the writing going on in the latter's classroom. Focused pairs are often initiated by the writing specialist, who takes the leadership role in the beginning. These arrangements are quite flexible and easy to manage, and they are generally pleasant affairs because the researchers often know and respect each other before undertaking the project. Focused pairs, in many cases, produce not only professional growth and change but also publications.

An example of a long-standing and productive focused pair is Barbara Walvoord, a writing specialist at Loyola College in Maryland, and Virginia Johnson Gazzam, a biologist at Towson State University. Walvoord and Gazzam first met in 1982 in a Maryland Writing Project WAC workshop that Walvoord led, and soon thereafter Walvoord invited Gazzam to collaborate with her in studying students' writing processes in Gazzam's biology classes. Gazzam has all the qualities that Walvoord says she looks for in a collaborator: She is self-confident, stable in her career (tenured like Walvoord), dependable, and productive. And, equally important, Walvoord saw that Gazzam was a committed and curious teacher who asked tough questions about her students' writing and about her own teaching. Gazzam wanted to know why her students didn't write up their experiments better and what they meant when they told her, "The writing you have us do is different from what we've been taught, different from what we do in English." In addition, Walvoord saw that Gazzam was interested not only in her own classroom but also in the larger theoretical issues of writing and learning that had been discussed in the workshop. Thus, this collaboration began, as many satisfying ones do, with two equal-status professionals agreeing to explore answers to questions they both cared a great deal about.

Since 1982, Walvoord and Gazzam have conducted naturalistic research in Gazzam's upper-division biology classrooms. In order to answer their questions about what Gazzam's students do between the time she makes the assignment and the time they hand in their final reports, Walvoord and Gazzam have collected the following kinds of data: (1) all students' notes, drafts, and final papers, (2) students' writing activity logs, (3) tapes of students interviewing each other about their processes and problems, (4) tapes of students' small-group meetings, and (5) tapes of students thinking aloud at home or in the dorm as they work on the experiment and the report. In addition, Walvoord has observed and participated in Gazzam's classes, interviewed her, and collected all of her instructional materials. As they have analyzed these data together, Walvoord and Gazzam have been able to glimpse what happens in students' minds as they fulfill Gazzam's assignment. Walvoord's and Gazzam's discoveries as they have gone along have refined their questions and, at times, redirected their research focus. These discoveries have also changed Gazzam's teaching.

Walvoord and Gazzam have given numerous conference presentations together in both of their disciplines, and these presentations have been, they say, extremely helpful to their collaboration. Going to conferences has given them time (on airplanes and over breakfast, for example) to reflect on their work, and presenting together has required them to agree on a common language for reporting their research. Furthermore, they say, each has gained insight into the other's disciplinary community, its language, concerns, and practitioners. Walvoord's and Gazzam's oral presentations have laid the foundation for their chapter in Walvoord and others (in press).

Walvoord speculates that the naturalistic (qualitative) research that she and Gazzam do together may be even more challenging for collaborators than research done in the experimental (quantitative) tradition. This is because naturalistic research is less structured, its questions and directions emerging as researchers gather and analyze data. Walvoord remembers one afternoon, shortly after they began data analysis, sitting in her den with Gazzam, the two of them looking at "about 400 pages of material and twenty hours of tapes." She turned to Gazzam and asked, "What shall we do now?" At times like those, Walvoord said, "You've got to be able to agree on analytic procedures, categories, and language; you've got to enjoy thinking together. Of course there will be conflict. That's what you want. That's what makes it rich. But you have to have strategies for *negotiating* conflict. And a sense of humor doesn't hurt." Walvoord's and Gazzam's collaboration, like other satisfying ones we've heard about, has become richer over time as the researchers have come to understand and perceive through each other's perspective.

Other collaborative studies of writing across the curriculum that may be characterized as focused-pair research include Flynn (1987), writing and chemical engineering; Flynn, McCulley, and Gratz (1986), writing and biology; Forman and Katsky (1986), writing and social psychology; Gorman, Gorman, and Young (1986), psychology and writing; Maimon and Nodine (1978), writing and psychology; McCarthy and Braffman (1985), writing and history; Neubert and McNelis (1986), education and English; Selfe and Arbabi (1986), writing and civil engineering; Selfe, Petersen, and Nahrgang (1986), writing and mathematics; Singer and Walvoord (1984), business and writing; Soven and Sullivan (1987), writing and philosophy; Strauss and Fulwiler (1987), chemistry and writing; Walvoord and others (in press), writing and biology, history, production management, and psychology. About one third of these studies are experimental and two thirds are naturalistic.

Collaborative Research Model 2: The Reciprocal Pair. This structure is unlike the focused pair in which both researchers investigate writing in the discipline teacher's classroom. Instead, in this model, two teacher-researchers exchange classroom visits, exploring the writing going on in both contexts. Reciprocal pairings are often initiated by a group of which the researchers are a part, a group that may help the researchers manage their project by providing release time. Reciprocal collaborations, perhaps even more than collaborations of other types, may require scheduled release time for pairs to plan and carry out each visit and then discuss it afterward (Neubert and Binko, 1987).

In 1986, the Philadelphia Writing Project initiated a program of reciprocal pairings for secondary teachers. In addition to adequate release time (and excellent substitute teachers), successful reciprocal-pair collaboration depends, according to project director Susan Lytle, on the teacher-researchers' controlling their own relationships. If teachers are to become "expert learners" together, they must feel that they are having observations done *for* them, not *to* them. Thus, it is important that the teachers being observed initiate the visits, inviting the visitor into their classrooms in order to obtain help on a particular problem. The teacher being observed should also suggest the most helpful role for the visitor to play: observer, student, team teacher, or solo teacher demonstrating a writing-related lesson.

Philadelphia Writing Project pairs consist of one member trained as a teacher-consultant in the project's summer institute and one member not so trained. Teacher-consultants meet regularly to share the journals they keep about their reciprocal visits, journals that focus on the process of teachers influencing each other. Although most pairings at the secondary level have included at least one English teacher, this need not necessarily be the case and will change soon, according to Lytle, as more discipline teachers are trained to be teacher-consultants. Several conference presentations have resulted from this program (Philadelphia Writing Project, 1987).

Reciprocal pairings at the college level were part of a five-year WAC program funded by the National Endowment for the Humanities (NEH) at Loyola College in Maryland. In this program, completed in 1986, pairs of teachers, all consisting of a writing specialist and a discipline teacher, were given release time for a semester to attend a course taught by their partner. The same group of students had been scheduled into each pair of observed classes. During a summer workshop preceding the reciprocal observations, paired teachers worked together, deciding on ways to combine their subject matters for their shared students and on roles they would play in each other's classes. During the semester of their collaboration, nearly all pairs responded together to students' papers. This was "a sobering experience," writing teacher Barbara Mallonee told us, when she gave a paper a B and her historian collaborator John Breihan gave the same paper a D. In the process of articulating what they were rewarding, these teachers learned more about their own notions of "good" writing. Each of them also learned to value things that they had previously regarded as peripheral, and this influenced their teaching. In coauthoring an article (Mallonee and Breihan, 1985) about the insights they gained from reading student papers together, this pair exchanged drafts of their manuscript and, at times, composed together, sitting side by side at the word processor. When they could not agree on ideas or language, they actually composed alternate sentences. The voice that emerged, Mallonee said, belonged to neither of them; rather, it was a composite that pleased them both.

In another Loyola College reciprocal pairing, structured like Mallonee's and Breihan's, Judith Dobler, a writing specialist, and Faith Gilroy, a psychologist, shared twenty-five students and exchanged classroom visits for a semester. Dobler met these twenty-five students in her freshman composition class in the morning while Gilroy observed, and Gilroy met them in the afternoon for social psychology while Dobler observed. Writing instruction was integrated with psychology instruction in ways the pair had agreed on during the previous summer's workshop. As a result of their reciprocal observations and subsequent discussions, both said, they came to understand more fully the writing and learning in their own and the other's classroom.

At the end of the semester, Dobler and Gilroy combined research methods from their disciplines in order to answer questions that had emerged during their classroom observations. As they had scrutinized students' work in social psychology, Dobler and Gilroy had been surprised at how difficult it was for their students to read psychology journals and how much time students spent on assigned articles. Thus, in order to understand better the task of reading in psychology, Dobler and Gilroy combined text analysis and an attitude survey to compare the prose styles of various psychology journals with the attitudes of professional psychologists and students toward these journals (Dobler and Gilroy, 1987). This pair's successful research experience supports Odell's (1987) contention that, ultimately, "the best research question is one that arises from an area in which [the researchers] are interested and with which [they] have experience; the best analytic procedures are those that [researchers] modify or invent to answer [their] own questions" (p. 137).

Collaborative Model 3: The Chief Researcher with Many Collaborators and Informants. In this model, a single researcher or a group of researchers pursues the answers to research questions into whatever settings they lead and the researcher or group works with whatever collaborators or informants can help. Informants are distinguished from collaborators in that informants only provide information to researchers while collaborators, though they may also provide information, help the chief researcher plan and carry out the research. In this model, students can and *should* play both roles, their perspectives as informants and collaborators being sought at every stage of the research. This is because students bring a perspective to both data collection and analysis that is very different from the perspective of teacher-researchers. Those who have collaborated with students say that students' insights are invaluable (Goswami, personal communication, October 1987). Projects that fit into this model are usually initiated by an individual or an institution, and data collection extends over a long period of time.

An example of this collaborative structure is found in a two-stage project begun in 1978 at Canisius College by chief researcher David Lauerman (1988; Lauerman, Schroeder, Sroka, and Stephenson, 1985). In the first stage, Lauerman and several colleagues in the English department conducted research into writing in nonacademic settings—in business, government and the social services, science and technology, and teaching and "public life" (the media, public relations, law, and fund raising). They involved faculty members from other disciplines by asking them what professions their majors chose and the names of people to contact in those professions (often Canisius alumni). Faculty across the disciplines were also invited, after the research was concluded, to participate in a workshop where Lauerman and his colleagues shared their findings about writing in these nonacademic settings and began to define goals for upper-level writing courses aimed at business, social science, science, education, and humanities majors. Also invited to participate in these workshops were the project's informants—that is, the business and professional people whose writing had been studied. After the workshops, members of the English department worked out final course designs. About this project Lauerman told us, "Our research in writing across the curriculum is a queer bird. The writing that people are doing in the community informs the writing that our students do on campus. Usually people in academia see it the other way around" (personal communication, October 1987).

Of equal interest is the second stage of the Canisius College project. Here Lauerman continues to play the role of chief researcher, but now he manages a research team comprised of the students in his classes. Lauerman's students, using the same research methods that Lauerman and his English department colleagues used in the first stage—namely, questionnaires, text analysis, and discourse-based interviews (Odell, Goswami, and Herrington, 1983)—carry out research into writing in settings of their own choice. According to Lauerman, students' research activities are central to his courses and are vivid and exciting learning experiences for students. They discover, as they conduct research, what it is that writers in particular settings actually do, what these writers know, and what constraints they must deal with. It is this research component in his writing courses, Lauerman believes, that keeps them oversubscribed semester after semester. And not only do students value the research but administrators and faculty in business and other disciplines also value and recommend it. Administrators and faculty's confidence in the English department's writing courses came originally, Lauerman says, from their participation in the research process.

Additional studies that may be characterized as following the model of the chief researcher with many collaborators and informants include Applebee, Auten, and Lehr (1981), Biddle and Fulwiler (in press), Britton and others (1975), Herrington (1985) Martin, D'Arcy, Newton, and Parker (1976), McCarthy (1987), Nelson (1987), and the Sociology Writing Group (1986).

Research Design and Methods

A detailed discussion of research design and methods cannot be undertaken in this chapter. Here we are limited to recommending a few sources that we feel provide helpful discussions of theories and methods of classroom research. Many of the sources we recommend emphasize naturalistic approaches that study writing in context. We suggest these sources because of researchers' increasing appreciation of the central role that social context plays in shaping writers' processes and products and in defining their successes and failures. We would like to caution, however, that just reading about various research methodologies is not likely to be enough. As Odell points out, "such reading will probably have to be supplemented by frequent conversations with someone who understands both research methodology and the goals of a specific study" (1987, p. 135).

Excellent theoretical and practical introductions to classroom research are provided by Goswami and Stillman (1987) and Myers (1985). The ethnographic approach is discussed by Doheny-Farina and Odell (1985), Gilmore and Glatthorn (1982), Hymes (1972), Spindler (1982), and Spradley (1979, 1980). Survey methodology is discussed by Anderson (1985). And issues of reliability and validity in naturalistic research are dealt with in Goetz and LeCompte (1984) and Lincoln and Guba (1985).

Conclusion

Collaborative research, undertaken to answer teachers' questions about their own and their students' practices is, we believe, an essential component of writing across the curriculum's second stage. This research is based on the assumption that knowledge is gained not only through action but also for action. For many of the teacher-researchers we talked to, their collaborative research represents a highly valued learning process. Their systematic research in writing across the curriculum has yielded insights that are both intellectually exciting and personally renewing for them. And these insights are the necessary foundation for lasting and satisfying change.

References

Anderson, P. V. "Survey Methodology." In L. Odell and D. Goswami (eds.), *Writing in Nonacademic Settings.* New York: Guilford, 1985.

Applebee, A. N., Auten, A., and Lehr, F. *Writing in the Secondary School.* Urbana, Ill.: National Council of Teachers of English, 1981.

Biddle, A., and Fulwiler, T. "The Community of Scholars in Our Own Backyard." *ADE Bulletin,* in press.

Britton, J., Burgess, T., Martin, N., McLeod, A., and Rosen, H. *The Development of Writing Abilities (11-18).* London: Macmillan, 1975.

Bruffee, K. "Collaborative Learning and the 'Conversation of Mankind.' " *College English,* 1984, *46* (7), 635-652.

Dobler, J. M., and Gilroy, F. D. "Psychology of the Scientist: LV. Social Psychologists' Perceptions of Journals' Readability: How Consistent Are They?" *Perceptual and Motor Skills,* 1987, *65,* 231-238.

Doheny-Farina, S., and Odell, L. "Ethnographic Research on Writing: Assumptions and Methodology." In L. Odell and D. Goswami (eds.), *Writing in Nonacademic Settings.* New York: Guilford, 1985.

Flynn, E. A. "Revising Writing Across the Curriculum: Reading and Writing Processes of Four Students in a Chemical Engineering Plant Design Course." Paper presented at the Conference on College Composition and Communication, Atlanta, March 1987.

Flynn, E. A., McCulley, G. A., and Gratz, R. K. "Writing in Biology: Effects of Peer Critiquing and Analysis of Models on the Quality of Biology Laboratory Reports." In A. Young and T. Fulwiler (eds.), *Writing Across the Disciplines: Research into Practice.* Upper Montclair, N.J.: Boynton/Cook, 1986.

Forman, J., and Katsky, P. "The Group Report: A Problem in Small-Group or Writing Processes?" *Journal of Business Communication,* 1986, *23* (4), 23-35.

Gilmore, P., and Glatthorn, A. (eds.). *Children in and out of School: Ethnography and Education.* Washington, D.C.: Center for Applied Linguistics, 1982.

Goetz, J., and LeCompte, M. *Ethnographic and Qualitative Design in Educational Research.* New York: Academic Press, 1984.

Gorman, M. E., Gorman, M. E., and Young, A. "Poetic Writing in Psychology." In A. Young and T. Fulwiler (eds.), *Writing Across the Disciplines: Research into Practice.* Upper Montclair, N.J.: Boynton/Cook, 1986.

Goswami, D., and Stillman, P. (eds.). *Reclaiming the Classroom: Teacher Research as an Agency for Change.* Upper Montclair, N.J.: Boynton/Cook, 1987.

Herrington, A. "Writing in Academic Settings: A Study of the Contexts for Writing in Two College Chemical Engineering Courses." *Research in the Teaching of English,* 1985, *19* (3), 331-359.

Hymes, D. "Introduction." In C. Cazden, V. P. John, and D. Hymes (eds.), *Functions of Language in the Classroom.* New York: Teachers College Press, 1972.

Lauerman, D. A. "Building Ethos: Field Research as a Design Feature in a Business Communications Course." In M. Kogen (ed.), *Writing in the Business Professions.* Urbana, Ill.: National Council of Teachers of English, 1988.

Lauerman, D. A., Schroeder, M. W., Sroka, K., and Stephenson, E. R. "Workplace and Classroom: Principles for Designing Writing Courses." In L. Odell and D. Goswami (eds.), *Writing in Nonacademic Settings.* New York: Guilford, 1985.

Lincoln, Y., and Guba, E. *Naturalistic Inquiry.* Newbury Park, Calif.: Sage, 1985.

McCarthy, L. P. "A Stranger in Strange Lands: A College Student Writing Across the Curriculum." *Research in the Teaching of English,* 1987, *21* (3), 233-265.

McCarthy, L. P., and Braffman, E. J. "Creating Victorian Philadelphia: Children Reading and Writing the World." *Curriculum Inquiry,* 1985, *15* (2), 122-151.

Maimon, E. P., and Nodine, B. "Measuring Syntactic Growth: Errors and Expectations in Sentence-Combining Practice with College Freshmen." *Research in the Teaching of English,* 1978, *12* (3), 233-244.

Mallonee, B. C., and Breihan, J. R. "Responding to Students' Drafts: Interdisciplinary Consensus." *College Composition and Communication,* 1985, *36* (2), 213-231.

Martin, N., D'Arcy, P., Newton, B., and Parker, R. *Writing and Learning Across the Curriculum, 11-16.* Upper Montclair, N.J.: Boynton/Cook, 1976.

Myers, M. *The Teacher-Researcher: How to Study Writing in the Classroom.* Urbana, Ill.: National Council of Teachers of English, 1985.

Nelson, M. "Increasing the Rigor of Teacher Research—A Cumulative Collaborative Model." Paper presented at the National Council of Teachers of English Research Assembly, San Francisco, November 1987.

Neubert, G., and Binko, J. "Using Peer Coaching to Improve College Teaching."

Paper presented at the American Educational Research Association Conference, Washington, D.C., April 1987.

Neubert, G., and McNelis, S. "Gender Interaction During High School Writing Response Groups." Paper presented at the National Council of Teachers of English Convention, San Antonio, Texas, November 1986.

Odell, L. "Planning Classroom Research." In D. Goswami and P. Stillman (eds.), *Reclaiming the Classroom: Teacher Research as an Agency for Change.* Upper Montclair, N.J.: Boynton/Cook, 1987.

Odell, L., Goswami, D., and Herrington, A. "The Discourse-Based Interview: A Procedure for Exploring the Tacit Knowledge of Writers in Nonacademic Settings." In P. Mosenthal, L. Tamor, and S. Walmsley (eds.), *Research on Writing.* New York: Longman, 1983.

Philadelphia Writing Project. *Work in Progress.* Philadelphia: Graduate School of Education, University of Pennsylvania, 1987.

Selfe, C. L., and Arbabi, F. "Writing to Learn: Engineering Student Journals." In A. Young and T. Fulwiler (eds.), *Writing Across the Disciplines: Research into Practice.* Upper Montclair, N.J.: Boynton/Cook, 1986.

Selfe, C. L., Petersen, B. T., and Nahrgang, C. L. "Journal Writing in Mathematics." In A. Young and T. Fulwiler (eds.), *Writing Across the Disciplines: Research into Practice.* Upper Montclair, N.J.: Boynton/Cook, 1986.

Singer, D., and Walvoord, B. "Process-Oriented Writing Instruction in a Case-Method Class." In J. A. Pierce and R. B. Robinson (eds.), *Proceedings of the Academy of Management.* Boston: Academy of Management, 1984. (ED 249 500)

Sociology Writing Group. *A Guide to Writing Sociology Papers.* New York: St. Martin's Press, 1986.

Soven, M., and Sullivan, W. "Writing to Learn: Assessing the Impact of Different Approaches to Philosophy." Paper presented at the Conference on Interpretive Communities and the Undergraduate Writer, University of Chicago, May 1987.

Spindler, G. *Doing the Ethnography of Schooling: Educational Anthropology in Action.* New York: Holt, Rinehart & Winston, 1982.

Spradley, J. *The Ethnographic Interview.* New York: Holt, Rinehart & Winston, 1979.

Spradley, J. *Participant Observation.* New York: Holt, Rinehart & Winston, 1980.

Strauss, M. J., and Fulwiler, T. "Interactive Writing and Learning in Chemistry." *Journal of College Science Teaching,* 1987, *26* (4), 256-262.

Wallat, C., Green, J. L., Conlin, S. M., and Haramis, M. "Issues Related to Action Research in the Classroom—The Teacher and Researcher as a Team." In J. L. Green and C. Wallat (eds.), *Ethnography and Language in Educational Settings.* Norwood, N.J.: Ablex, 1981.

Walvoord, B. E., and Dowling, H. F. "The Baltimore Area Consortium." In T. Fulwiler and A. Young (eds.), *Writing Across the Curriculum: Programs, Practices, and Problems.* Portsmouth, N. H.: Boynton/Cook, in press.

Walvoord, B. E., McCarthy, L. P., Breihan, J. R., Gazzam, V., Robinson, S. M., and Sherman, A. K. *Thinking and Writing in College.* Urbana, Ill.: National Council of Teachers of English, in press.

Lucille Parkinson McCarthy is an assistant professor of English and teaches writing at the University of Maryland Baltimore County; in 1986 she received the Promising Researcher Award from the National Council of Teachers of English.

Barbara E. Walvoord is an associate professor of writing at Loyola College in Maryland and is a founder and former codirector of the Maryland Writing Project and the Baltimore Area Consortium for Writing Across the Curriculum. She is also a member of the board of consultants of the National Network of Writing Across the Curriculum Programs.

Continuing problems, troubling trends, and many
opportunities face WAC planners as we look to the future.
How can we deal with these in order to sustain the success
of the movement?

The Future of Writing
Across the Curriculum

Christopher Thaiss

It's impossible for me to talk about the future without first estimating where writing across the curriculum is now. Many ideas fit under the WAC umbrella. At more and more schools, WAC means the writing-intensive or writing-emphasis courses taught within a major. This can imply careful instruction in the phases of the writing process—discovery, revision, and editing—or it can merely mean increasing the required word count in a course. At many schools, including some of those with writing-emphasis courses, WAC means teachers in diverse fields using writing-to-learn techniques, such as journals, reading response logs, systematic note making, impromptu exercises, role playing, field studies, I-Search papers, collaborative research, informal and formal debates, process analyses, formative assessments, and so on.

Writing across the curriculum also means research. Curiosity drives the vanguard. Although many of us got into this movement (it is, for all our modest disclaimers, messianic) because someone in our institution consulted us based on our experience as teachers of writing, we stick with it because we quickly see the limits of our knowledge and find, humbly and gratefully, that we can learn a lot about our profession from the people "out there," teachers in other fields. The collaborative research projects described in Chapter Eight raise to the level of art the spontane-

S. H. McLeod (ed.). *Strengthening Programs for Writing Across the Curriculum.*
New Directions for Teaching and Learning, no. 36. San Francisco: Jossey-Bass, Winter 1988.

ous collaborations that ideally go on in every cross-curricular workshop—indeed, in any earnest exchange of ideas and questions among teachers.

The cross-curricular urge is not, in my view, an offshoot of the teaching of writing but is its foundation. We can't know what and how to teach unless we mess around in the beautiful muck of people's texts and their purposes, backgrounds, fears, fantasies, and delusions in regard to writing. And to do this we must go outside the boundaries of our departments and beyond the fringe parking of our campuses.

I talk as if this is simple truth, but I realize how revolutionary—and evolutionary—it is. People who enjoy studying writing across the curriculum in its myriad guises, or writing in the workplace, or the composing processes of young children are people who marvel at the diversity and unpredictability of culture. These are not the same people who think of "writing across the curriculum" as a mandate to impose a single standard of syntactical correctness or a short list of required readings across the curriculum. Those, I would argue, are antithetical meanings of the concept and reasons why the term occasions resistance and confusion. Most of the WAC people one meets have swum around in cultural stews throughout their careers. We tend to be the ESL people, the writing center people, the pop culturists, the Third World historians, the Geertzian anthropologists, the quantum physicists, the epidemiologists, the systems engineers—entrepreneurs of every stripe.

We have seen that using language can empower people, enable them to survive in body and flourish in spirit. We have seen how the force to limit communication—whether that force takes the form of monopoly in mass media or the radical narrowing of standards of "acceptable language"—can intimidate, passify (not pacify), and disenfranchise people. Yes, writing across the curriculum advocates want people to write about whatever they study, because they see writing as power, whether that power be political or spiritual or therapeutic or intellectual.

WAC has succeeded because workshop participants have felt this power themselves in the workshops and then in their classrooms. They have reached the same insights as those achieved by such writing-process researchers as Emig (1977) and Shaughnessy (1977), who convinced our profession more than a decade ago that writing is learning and growth, that the act of writing defines writing, and that no text is more than a step in anyone's development. WAC would never have spread had its advocates had nothing more to offer fellow teachers than correction symbols, syntax rules, and pious lectures about the need for "good" writing. When workshop participants praise their experience, they always focus on how writing serves intellectual and social purposes: "I feel that I understand my students better," "Writing gives them an outlet for their confusion, their frustrations," "They reach insights I never hoped for before." Not surprisingly, as Shaughnessy predicted in *Errors and Expec-*

tations, teachers also see gains in the quality of student texts: "They write a lot better than previous classes."

As we confront trends and issues in planning new and continuing WAC programs, we need to keep in mind the bases of our success: our desire to learn from our colleagues and our sense of the power of writing. It is on these strengths that we can build the future of the movement.

The Future of WAC: Two Troubling Trends

Ironically, as I look to the future of WAC, our very success troubles me. Just as "the writing process," through the perseverance of many teachers and researchers, has become so successful that now almost everyone in our field slaps the name onto whatever they do, so the term "writing across the curriculum" stands in danger of the same thing. Two trends need to be watched closely: the textbook-title syndrome and the top-down decree.

The Textbook-Title Syndrome. When I review manuscripts with "across the curriculum" or "in the content areas" or "across the disciplines" in the title, I've learned to ask a simple question: What makes the book different from the books published before the "across the curriculum" furor began? A disappointingly large number have merely substituted sample essays about physics, sociology, and computers for such previous staples as E. B. White's trip to the lake, Annie Dillard's sojourn at the creek, or John Updike's idyll of the grocery store. Though they provide different grist for the composition mill, such "content area" essays still exist as static texts, imposing for their polish and learnedness while the processes of their writers remain opaque. Such textbooks assume, as their predecessors did, that the composition course stands isolated from the rest of the curriculum. If it did not, then students in the composition course would write about what they are reading, hearing, discussing—and writing—in the other courses they actually take. They wouldn't need a book full of assorted essays.

Indeed, I feel that such texts can actually hinder writing across the curriculum more than they promote it. The student who must write about Loren Eiseley or Stephen Jay Gould in the composition class will not have the chance to get her or his peers' or the writing teacher's feedback on the draft of the research paper she is writing in cell biology. Even those textbooks that present samples closer to the actual college curriculum (for example, sample lab reports, field studies, or business case analyses written by students) essentially privilege static texts that have very little to do with the actual classes our students are taking now. If faculty at an institution really talk with their colleagues on the next floor or in the next building and if they take steps to find out what their students are really studying and writing in their other classes, then there is no need for any teacher or publisher to have to fabricate reading matter, topics, purposes, or audiences for their students. If our message is that "writing is important in every field," then what better way to show this than by taking seriously in the writing class the writing that the students really must do?

If you suspect that your students are not writing in their other classes (many teachers use a student questionnaire to find this out), then that "cross-curricular" textbook won't convince students that they should be. Yet even if students are not writing on assignment in those classes, they are still reading, hearing lectures, perhaps doing hands-on work, and taking notes (so they *are* writing). You can turn your writing class into a writing across the curriculum class by teaching your students such writing-to-learn strategies as double-entry note making, reading response logs, and I-Search papers, using the readings and lectures from their other classes as topics. Meanwhile, you can be politicking for more WAC faculty development workshops on your campus.

The Top-Down Decree. The other problem with success is that administrators try to decree it by decreeing WAC programs, rather than by assisting the growth of grassroots efforts. One assumption on which this sourcebook is based is that some faculty development, primarily voluntary, should precede legislated or decreed changes in curriculum. The activities described in Chapter Two presuppose a cross-disciplinary core of faculty who have already understood some writing-process and writing-to-learn theory. This core need not be large. Every faculty has at least a few, maybe many, teachers who quickly pick up the spirit of the workshop, probably because of their own experience as writers or because, like many teachers I've met, they are already using writing-to-learn or process techniques in their classes. Without these people—and without some faculty development structure to spread their ideas—faculty are liable to think that "WAC" merely means: (1) "adding the English teacher's job" to theirs or (2) "adding writing" to their courses.

At our meetings of the National Network of Writing Across the Curriculum Programs and in my conversations with program directors, I keep hearing the same lament about mandated WAC curricula, particularly of the writing-intensive or writing-emphasis variety. Several large public universities, plus many smaller schools, have decreed such programs, in some cases without prior faculty development, sometimes even without faculty debate and consent. Often faculty resist, and those in charge either can't meet their quota of writing-intensive sections or are forced to accept as writing intensive some sections taught by faculty who don't know how to handle student writing but who understandably want the usual reward of reduced class size or release time. Let me suggest, first of all, that the granting of such rewards reinforces the misconception that writing is additive, not instrumental. Experienced WAC folks know that sensibly using writing as a mode of learning in classes does not mean that we reach fewer students or expend more time in teaching; it just means that teaching and learning occur more efficiently.

Another common complaint concerns students: They'll tolerate the one or two writing courses they need to graduate, but woe to the teacher who requires writing in any other course! As long as writing is presented as the production of more words, rather than as an essential tool of thought, then we can only expect that students will resent it as an imposition.

Suggestions for Resisting These Trends. If mandatory WAC, either through decreed writing-intensive courses in the majors, through committee selection of a so-called writing across the curriculum anthology, or through some other expedient, is considered by a college or department before a cross-campus enthusiastic core of faculty has been developed, we should resist it, even though it might appear to represent an administrative commitment to writing. We need to keep pointing out to administrators that every WAC program that has endured and flourished was built on a firm basis of faculty development before sweeping changes in requirements were made.

As for compensation, rather than doling out release time and reduced student loads to faculty who teach writing-intensive courses, spend the release time or some other suitable reward on faculty development workshops and on continuing coordination of the faculty development program. The same amount of money or time that is spent to support the same small percentage of writing-intensive courses could be spent each year instead to train new faculty in writing-process and writing-to-learn techniques, with a far greater payoff. In doing so, the number of trained faculty will increase continually, hence the number of potential WAC sections will increase as well. Under this plan, there is no limit to the spread of WAC in the institution; moreover, students will not regard writing requirements as extraordinary, because no classes will be identified exclusively as "writing-intensive."

As for text selection, keep in mind that no externally published text can give your faculty working knowledge of their colleagues' courses, assignments, and ways of dealing with student writing. Questioning fellow faculty from other departments or assigning your students to conduct interviews with their other teachers will give you better data about writing across the curriculum than any anthology. Anyone experienced in cross-disciplinary workshops has learned that what is asked of students in writing and how the teacher handles it can vary drastically from one course or one teacher to another within the same subject.

For a writing across the curriculum course itself, choose texts that help you teach students ways to identify each of their "discourse communities" during the current semester, rather than assigning them any anthology's homogenized ideas about "writing in science" or "writing in the humanities." If your current text teaches writing-to-learn techniques and if it helps students understand the writing process so that they write discovery drafts, get good feedback, and revise, don't change it. Understanding the process of writing and how to use writing to learn will allow students to handle any form, format, or criterion a teacher may throw at them, regardless of the discipline.

Other Issues in the Future of WAC

Cultural Literacy or "Method" Versus "Content." This is not an issue of the future, really, since WAC people have always had to answer the skepticism of faculty who see the time devoted to writing-to-learn activities as time taken away from the teaching of content. We have always had to confront the unexamined notion that people learn any body of information (whether the names of Greek philosophers or the lyrics of a rock song) merely by being given a text and being told to read it, or by having someone stand before a class and tell it to them. What is new is the slick term "cultural literacy" and the facile coupling of this boost for a certain list of names, events, and abstract terms with an attack on schools' alleged overemphasis on methods of learning.

Those who have studied writing and learning across the curriculum—to use Nancy Martin's (Martin, D'Arcy, Newton, and Parker, 1976) still-incisive phrase—know, of course, that real attention to how we learn has always taken a backseat to schools' and colleges' concern about the books required and the content of lectures. College faculty discover that students can't match dates with events and that they look puzzled when classic authors are mentioned. Faculty therefore assume that students were never told about the events and were never required to read Shakespeare or Hawthorne. Even a brief look at high school curricula, however, would tell college teachers that all the stuff was in the books and on the syllabus but that it somehow didn't become part of students' knowledge (or, if it did, the college teacher just hasn't used enough writing-to-learn exercises to access it!). After more than twenty years of research in what James Britton (1970) called "language and learning," we know that it is method that makes the difference. Content and method are not opposed; one is the means to the other. To place them in opposition is to assert, ironically, that the content is not worth achieving.

There is no better way to achieve cultural literacy (or cross-cultural literacy or intercultural literacy) than through writing to learn. A WAC workshop could even be called "The Pragmatics of Cultural Literacy," if that is your interest. And if you want to cite classical precedents for your methodology, they are everywhere. Is there a better example of a language-intensive class than that of Socrates? All those teachers who just lectured their students have been forgotten; Socrates, the expert and patient discussion leader, has continued to teach through the ages. And how does he continue to teach? Through the student, Plato, who kept the most complete learning log. If it weren't for Plato's writing in order to understand the intense debates led by his mentor, would we even have a Greek philosophical "content" to talk about? Without the "thinkwriting" of a Newton or Darwin or . . . well, you can see what I mean.

General Education Reform. Though colleges and universities continually tinker with required courses, enthusiams for general education reform has been fueled by Secretary of Education Bennett in Washington, by privately funded studies and association reports, and, most recently, by the cultural literacy debate. Much WAC activity has come about as part of institutions' desire to upgrade students' writing, and this improvement has been seen as a task of the general education curriculum. Rarely (there are exceptions) does a school undertake a writing across the disciplines effort unless it already has what it considers to be a strong freshman composition course or unless it creates one. Happily, almost all faculties now see written communication as a vital component of any core. A primary goal of WAC in the future should be to make writing to learn as widely accepted.

I would urge any WAC planner, if he or she is not already part of the institution's general education or core curriculum committee, to politick for membership. Such membership offers a wonderful opportunity to raise faculty consciousness about the essential link between writing and learning. And, if you are already a member of the committee, you are in the right position to suggest WAC alternatives to a ghettoized English composition course: (1) You can design a composition course that teaches writing-to-learn skills as well as drafting, peer feedback, and research techniques; (2) you can suggest pairing or clustering the writing course with other courses so that some assignments apply to more than one class; (3) you can suggest writing-to-learn techniques that suit each course in the core and that give students practice in a variety of skills; (4) you can argue the necessity of regular faculty development for general education teachers, and you can write the proposal for the funding of these workshops; and (5) you can counter every iteration of the content-or-method myth.

Cooperation Between Colleges and Secondary Schools. At last year's Virginia Conference on Language and Learning, a high school history teacher asked if college history teachers were doing things with writing to learn that she and her colleagues were trying in their classes. Though the answer was an emphatic yes, I realized that all disciplines face the same lack of across-levels communication among practitioners that we in English have always faced. Before WAC, college teachers of writing were concerned about what went on in the high school English classes their students had taken; high school teachers wanted to know the same about college English classes and customarily invited the local college composition director in for a chat. Now, as WAC succeeds in diffusing responsibility and spawning variety, it will be harder to isolate a spokesperson about an institution's writing program. Who can speak authoritatively about writing in the university after WAC workshops have been going on for several years? Who can represent "the writing program" at a WAC-inspired public high school?

If we accept both the intimate connection of writing and learning and the teacher's freedom to adapt WAC theory and strategies in new ways, then we can't ask a high school or a college for a definitive outline of required writing skills. I think we need to be forthright about this in our communication with secondary schools and make a virtue of necessity. Rather than pretend that there is consensus where there are only individuals experimenting and adapting, talk up the dynamic nature of the enterprise. Rather than pretend that you are the expert on your campus, list the names and numbers of your WAC nucleus. If you have gone the extra mile and have developed an in-house WAC newsletter (the National Network of Writing Across the Curriculum Programs has about fifty of these among its 500 member institutions), be sure to show copies to those who inquire about your program; the articles by teachers give substance to your anecdotes.

It will become important to use whatever liaison between your college and the schools that you have (for example, a National Writing Project site or another in-service or recertification program) as a launchpad for networking across the curriculum. Like Bernadette Glaze, the high school history chair who serves as assistant director of the Northern Virginia Writing Project and who has organized annual language and learning conferences in Virginia, take as your goal to find out what's going on in your area in both colleges and schools. Use the easiest means—newsletter, conferences, informal meetings between the WAC rep from a college department and the WAC rep from its high school counterpart—to get people talking. Knowing that college professors are using writing-process and writing-to-learn techniques can boost the high school's WAC effort, and vice versa. Ignore conventional prejudice that says that high school teachers can't change the teaching methods of college faculty. I've seen it happen many times on my own campus, and every other National Writing Project site tells similar stories.

WAC, LAC, and ?AC. From the inception of WAC, logic has exerted pressure on the narrowness of the concept. The British Schools Council research teams in the 1960s saw that the marvelous teaching they witnessed cultivated all modes of language. Robert Parker (Martin, D'Arcy, Newton, and Parker, 1976), the American coauthor of *Writing and Learning Across the Curriculum, 11–16* (still one of the best books in the field), has always insisted that the movement be called "language across the curriculum." Anyone who has been involved in WAC knows that the writing part works only if reading, talking, and listening work with it. That WAC has remained a viable term probably shows that we have not yet succeeded in freeing the concept from its association with the English composition course and from our preoccupation with the production of student texts.

Logic and experience demand that we go outside conventional associations and share our findings with those who have achieved expertise in other language areas, such as reading specialists and oral communication specialists. A few years ago, a book project (Thaiss and Suhor, 1984) allowed me to work closely with several speech specialists. We were surprised to learn from one another how many techniques we shared, yet how bound we were in our assumptions about the preeminence of the language area each represented. As language teachers, we saw how much we had to teach each other about our specific fields. I've had a similar experience the past two years in working with reading specialist Tom Estes (Estes and Vaughn, 1986) in a faculty development program for Blue Ridge Community College (Virginia).

Logic also demands that we listen to those colleagues who (sometimes facetiously) remark, "If we have writing across the curriculum, why not math and science across the curriculum?" Indeed, and why not music and economics and physical exercise? In a way, of course, such remarks beg the question: "Do you mean to imply that we don't already have these subjects across the curriculum?" Just as the WAC planner should never assume that writing process and writing to learn are *not* going on in unexpected places, so no other discipline specialist should assume that students are not learning important lessons about his or her field in a nonspecialist's classroom. One of the underemphasized spinoffs of the WAC workshop is that each of us learns a lot about other subjects—as long as all the participants get opportunities to demonstrate their teaching. And, as we learn from one another, we gradually reshape our teaching to accommodate the new and varied knowledge. I am no longer the same teacher of Shakespeare or of freshman composition that I was before I began to design general education courses with sociologists and global historians and natural scientists. They are not the same teachers they were before they heard about journals and practiced in-class writing. It's no wonder that the folks who meet at the WAC workshop show up again on the general education reform committee.

I think that WAC planners should expect, even hope, to see their programs merge into more broadly conceived interdisciplinary ventures. One way to measure the success of your WAC workshops is to see, over the years, how many other cross-curricular initiatives sprout up, from research projects to team-taught courses to general education reforms to grant proposals to degree programs to administrative offices. We have to be patient. We also have to abjure possessiveness. The longer we hold onto the WAC workshop as "our program" and the longer we stay chained to one format, the longer WAC will remain unassimilated.

Reports I hear through the network assure me that being willing to loosen the reins will not lead to our being thrown off. Indeed, as more and more people begin to own stock in branches of the endeavor, the calls for our experience become more frequent. Granted, those branches may not look like something we would have designed, but we have to live with the realization that inviting people into any workshop means that they will go off and do unique, sometimes disquieting things with the information. These variations are built into the model. Sometimes we will feel that we must intercede, as I, for example, sometimes do when a colleague's writing across the curriculum course appears to ignore process and just increase the required word count. Probably fortunately, we won't have time to intercede nearly as often as we would like. In talking with students, I have been surprised to learn how much they say they've benefited from writing assignments and teacher methods that I thought were misguided.

WAC and "Good Writing": Who's in Charge? In Chapter Four, Ellen Strenski raises the issue of style by describing a conflict between an English teacher and a teacher in another department, both of whom evaluated a student's paper. The other professor wanted technical language; the English professor wanted language for the layperson. To my mind, this shouldn't be an issue; it is an example of the success of WAC. The student felt the challenge of writing on the same topic for different audiences; how fortunate to have this experience before going into the business world! To demand that either teacher change criteria would falsify the experience and rob the student of a chance to learn.

While I say that conflicts in style should not be an issue, I realize that, as WAC proliferates and control of writing becomes diffused among departments (for example, through writing-intensive courses), students may encounter an even more bewildering variety of criteria than they would find in a non-WAC English sequence, where students always complain about inconsistency from teacher to teacher. If students do encounter a teacher who won't permit the first person, another who thrives on personal experience essays, a third who wants footnotes for every line, and a fourth who wants only original observations, lucky for them. That's the real world of writing, where tastes and formats differ wildly. If they get a sense of this from their WAC experience, hurray!

On the other hand, diffusion of responsibility and control may mean that the student of computer design or sociology or literary criticism might write only in a major-sponsored writing-intensive course, hence missing the fortunate frustration of writing for a teacher who doesn't know any of the jargon—one thing that can always be said for us composition teachers is that our students always have to write down to us! It is of no small concern to many teachers of writing in schools with writing-intensive programs that students will not get the important practice of translating specialized knowledge for a lay reader. This is potentially serious, since a frequent complaint about college graduates is that they can't communicate except with fellow specialists.

We can look at this situation positively. After all, it's better for students to do substantial writing in at least one or two courses than to do none at all, even if the vocabulary is esoteric and the writer does not have to defend the assumptions of the discipline to the reader. If the writing environment in the specific writing-intensive class is salutary, then students can use the experience to overcome writing anxiety and learn through the composing process. Thus, if the alternative is nothing, then "writing intensive only" is certainly preferable.

However, this potential hazard should inspire us to richer possibilities: First, we can argue for ongoing faculty development money, in lieu of release time for writing-intensive sections, in order to train new groups of teachers each year in a variety of writing-to-learn and writing-process techniques, hence varying the experiences for students. This method truly spreads writing across the curriculum. Second, we can opt for an upper-level required writing course, taught by faculty who are not specialists in the students' majors (the University of Maryland and George Mason University do this through the English department), in addition to the writing that students do in major courses. And, third, at the very least, this problem allows us to argue more convincingly for faculty development, including release time for one or more WAC specialists who can support the writing-intensive teachers by showing them how to vary audience for their students (for example, through the case method, through writing for outside readers, and through peer response groups).

Our Best Hopes: People and Writing

Though it's tempting to see our enterprise in terms of program models, teaching techniques, and course syllabi, the future of WAC, just like its present, depends on the imaginations and goodwill of people. The greatest thing we've got going for us is that people in every locale, every sort of school, and every subject area have become enthusiastic about the writing-learning connection. We may indeed have achieved a critical mass: I keep encountering teachers who've been using writing in their teaching for years—"I just started doing it one day and it worked"—and who only now are discovering that what they've been doing has been named—"I never called it anything, but I guess it was a learning log"—and that there are lots of other teachers who are equally excited about their success.

We have to remember to trust what we claim. We say that writing promotes thought, both critical and creative; we say that people who write about what they hear, read, and say come to fuller understanding. If we believe in these claims, then we can feel confident that WAC will continue to grow as long as people write and are encouraged to do so. Whatever else we have faculty do in our workshops, we must at least have them write. If we believe what we claim about writing, then the benefits of the writing will be so evident to our colleagues that they will need no push to share them with their students. Conversely, if participants do not feel these rewards, then no amount of pressure will spread writing across the curriculum, and the movement will vanish. This does not appear to be happening.

Further, I think we can also trust in the continued widening and intensifying of networks. People want to talk about these writing, learning, and teaching techniques; they want to write about them; they want to learn from others. Not a day goes by when I do not hear from two or three or six or more people, on my own campus and from all over the country, about what's going on in WAC. Nothing speaks so eloquently about the future of the movement as this frequent note: "I just wanted to let you know that I've asked for information from other people in the network. Everyone has been so willing to help."

References

Britton, J. *Language and Learning.* Harmondsworth, England: Pelican, 1970.

Emig, J. "Writing as a Mode of Learning." *College Composition and Communication,* 1977, *28,* 122–128.

Estes, T., and Vaughn, J. *Reading and Reasoning Beyond the Primary Grades.* Boston: Allyn & Bacon, 1986.

Martin, N., D'Arcy, P., Newton, B., and Parker, R. *Writing and Learning Across the Curriculum, 11–16.* Upper Montclair, N.J.: Boynton/Cook, 1976.

Shaughnessy, M. *Errors and Expectations.* New York: Oxford, 1977.

Thaiss, C., and Suhor, C. (eds.). *Speaking and Writing, K–12: Classroom Strategies and the New Research.* Urbana, Ill.: National Council of Teachers of English, 1984.

Christopher Thaiss is associate professor of English at George Mason University and coordinator of the National Network of Writing Across the Curriculum Programs.

APPENDIX

National Survey of Writing Across the Curriculum Programs

Conducted by Susan H. McLeod and compiled by Susan Shirley

In the fall of 1987, we sent a survey to all four-year and two-year colleges and universities in the United States and Canada. From it, we have compiled the following annotated list of writing across the curriculum programs, which we hope will be of use both to institutions seeking to start a WAC program and institutions needing advice about supporting fledgling programs. Surveys were mailed to 2,735 institutions; 1,112 were returned, 427 of which indicated that the institution has a WAC program in place. Those 427 programs are listed here. Since WAC programs are dynamic and evolve through the years, the components listed for each institution represent parts that have existed during the life of the program, although perhaps not at present. Listings are incomplete if surveys were returned to us with information missing. We thank the Department of English at Washington State University for its generous support of this project.

Key to Annotations

Contact name, department or program, institution, address, phone number.

Public or private institution (pub, priv)
Type of institution—community college (cc), four-year college (4 yr), M.A.-
    granting university (MA), Ph.D.-granting university (PhD)
Number of students (# stud)
WAC funding—external funding (ext), including (source), or internal funding
    (int fund).
Number of years (Number yrs) program has been in existence:
    (a) Just starting one
    (b) 1–2 years
    (c) 3–4 years
    (d) 5–6 years
    (e) 7–8 years or more.
Components (Comps) of WAC program:
    (a) A faculty seminar
    (b) Faculty workshops
    (c) Follow-up interviews or meetings with faculty
    (d) Writing fellows or TAs assigned to courses as writing coaches
    (e) A resident writing consultant
    (f) An all-university writing committee
    (g) A WAC advisory committee
    (h) In-house WAC publications
    (i) Informal but regular gatherings
    (j) Outside speakers or consultants
    (k) A writing lab or tutorials for students
    (l) Collaborative faculty research projects.
Curricular elements (Curr elem) of WAC program:
    (a) A WAC freshman composition course
    (b) Upper-division writing-intensive courses in the English department
    (c) Upper-division writing-intensive courses taught in other departments
    (d) Adjunct writing classes attached to courses in other disciplines.

Alabama

Margaret O. Broadnax, **Samford University**, Box 2205, Birmingham, AL 35229, (205) 870-2458. Priv, MS, 4,000 stud, int fund. Number yrs: c. Comps: e, f, k. Curr elem: a, b, c.

Gertrude Schroeder, Writing Ctr, **Troy State University**, Troy, AL 36082, (205) 566-3000 x305. Pub, MA, 4,000 stud, ext (Title III) & int fund. Number yrs: a. Comps: a, b, c, e, g, i, j, k. Curr elem: a, c, d.

Dorothy G. Grimes, English, Station 6432, **University of Montevallo**, Montevallo, AL 35115, (205) 665-6432. Pub, MA, 2,500 stud, int fund. Comps: a, b, f, j, k, l. Curr elem: a, c.

Lana Silverthorn, Director, USA Writing Program, **University of South Alabama**, Mobile, AL 36688, (205) 460-6480. Pub, MA, 10,000 stud, ext (NEH) & int fund. Number yrs: e. Comps: a, c, f, g, j, k. Curr elem: c.

Arizona

David E. Schwalm, English, **Arizona State University**, Tempe, AZ 85287, (602) 965-3853. Pub, PhD, 13,000 stud, ext (Ford Fdn) & int fund. Number yrs: a. Comps: a, b, d, f, g, j. Curr elem: c.

Barbara G. Hackett, **Glendale Community College**, 6000 W Olive Ave, Glendale, AZ 85302, (602) 435-3480. Pub, cc, 16,500 stud, int fund. Number yrs: c. Comps: b, e, k. Curr elem: a, d.

Paul J. Ferlazzo, English, **Northern Arizona State University**, Flagstaff, AZ 86011. Pub, PhD, 13,000 stud, ext (Ford Fdn) & int fund. Number yrs: a. Comps: c, d, e, g, j, k, l. Curr elem: c.

Stanley P. Witt, **Pima Community College**, 8202 E Poinciana Dr, Tucson, AZ 85730, (602) 886-3331. Pub, cc, 20,000 stud, ext (FIPSE) & int fund. Comps: b, c, d, g, h, j, k.

Julie Bertsch, **Rio Salado Community College, Maricopa District**, 640 N 1st Ave, Phoenix, AZ 85003, (602) 223-4205. Pub, cc, 70,000 stud, int fund. Number yrs: d. Comps: a, b, c, g, j, k.

Barbara Fahey Blakey, English, **Scottsdale Community College**, 9000 E Chaparral Rd, Scottsdale, AZ 85256, (602) 941-0999 x208. Pub, cc, 8,000 stud, int fund. Number yrs: c. Comps: b, c, d, e, h.

Arkansas

Virginia Wray, Humanities, **Arkansas College**, Batesville, AR 72501, (501) 793-9813 x347. Priv, 4 yr, 750 stud, int fund. Number yrs: b. Comps: d, e, k. Curr elem: a.

Larry Long, **Harding University**, Box 898, Station A, Searcy, AR 72143, (501) 268-6161 x421. Priv, 4 yr, 2,700 stud, int fund. Number yrs: a. Comps: a, c, k. Curr elem: a.

Alice Hines, **Hendrix College**, Box H-598, Conway, AR 72032, (501) 450-1244. Priv, 4 yr, 1,094 stud, int fund. Number yrs: a. Comps: a, b, c, i, j, k.

Mary Dement, **Mississippi County Community College**, Blytheville, AR 72315, (501) 762-1020. Pub, cc, 1,400 stud, int fund. Comps: b, d, e. Curr elem: a.

JoAnne Liebman, Director of Freshman Comp, English, **University of Arkansas, Little Rock**, AR 72204, (501) 569-3160. Int fund. Number yrs: c. Comps: a, c, j, k, l. Curr elem: b, d.

California

Daniel Cornell and Mark Sargent, English, **Biola University,** 13800 Biola Ave, La Mirada, CA 90639, (213) 944-0351. Priv, MA, 2,800 stud, int fund. Number yrs: a. Comps: b, c, f, g, k. Curr elem: c, e.

David R. Smith, 101-40, **California Institute of Technology,** Pasadena, CA 91125, (818) 356-3600. Int fund. Number yrs: a. Comps: d, g, k. Curr elem: d.

Janice Bowman, English, **California Lutheran College,** Thousand Oaks, CA 91360, (805) 493-3242. Priv, MA, 2,300 stud, ext (Kellogg Fdn) & int fund. Number years: e. Comps: a, b, c, d, e, h, i, k, l. Curr elem: a, d.

Kim Flachmann, English, **California State University, Bakersfield,** CA, 93311, (803) 833-3083. Pub, 4 yr, MA, 3,000 stud, int fund. Comps: a, c, e, h.

Edward M. White, English, **California State College, San Bernardino,** CA 92407, (714) 887-7493. Pub, MA, 8,000 stud, int fund. Comps: a, f, k. Curr elem: b, c.

Carol R. Holder, English, **California Polytechnic University,** 3801 West Temple Avenue, Pomona, CA 91766-4010, (714) 869-3833, 3940. Pub, MA, 19,000 stud, int fund. Number yrs: e. Comps: a, b, c, f, h, j, k, l.

Elizabeth Renfro, English, **California State University,** Mail stop, 830, **Chico,** CA 95929, (916) 895-4010, 6372. Pub, MA, 14,000 stud, int fund. Comps: a, b, c, e, f, g, h, j, k. Curr elem: c.

Thomas P. Klammer, English, **California State University, Fullerton,** CA 92634, (714) 773-3163. Pub, MA, 24,000 stud, int fund. Number yrs: e. Comps: a, f, k. Curr elem: c.

Thia Wolf, English, **California State University,** 18111 Nordhoff Street, **Northridge,** CA 91330, (818) 772-8408, 885-3431. Pub, MA, 30,000 stud, ext fund (state lottery). Number yrs: a. Comps: a, c, d, k. Curr elem: c.

Joan L. Maxwell, English, **California State University,** 6000 J Street, **Sacramento,** CA 95819, (916) 278-5732, 6409; 791-0739. Pub, 4 yr, MA, 18,000 stud, int fund. Number yrs: a. Comps: a, c, d, e, f, g. Curr elem: c, d.

Irene Plunkett Chowenhill and Cindy Hicks, Coords, Lang Arts, **Chabot College,** 25555 Hesperian Blvd, Hayward, CA 94540-5001, (415) 786-6804. Pub, cc, 18,800 stud, int fund. Comps: b, h, j, l. Curr elem: d.

Dorothy Augustine, English, **Chapman College,** Orange, CA 92666, (714) 997-6639, 6750. Priv, 4 yr, 1,200 stud, int fund. Comps: a, b, c, e, g, k. Curr elem: c.

James D. Collins, 800 College Avenue, **College of the Siskiyous,** Weed, CA 96094, (916) 938-4462. Pub, cc, 1,260 stud, int fund. Number yrs: c. Comps: b, d, j, k.

Dorothea Nudelman, **Foothill College,** Los Altos Hills, CA 94022, (415) 960-4436. Pub, cc, 13,000 stud, int fund. Number yrs: c. Comps: a, b, c, f, k.

Lois Powers, **Fullerton College,** 321 E Chapman, Fullerton, CA 92669, (714) 992-7451. Pub, cc, 16,000 stud, int fund. Number yrs: c. Comps: a, b, g, h.

Carolyn Brinkman, **Long Beach Community College,** 4901 E Carson St, Long Beach, CA 90808, (213) 420-4474. Pub, cc, 25,000 stud, ext & int fund. Number yrs: a. Comps: a, b, c, g, k.

Linda Bannister, English, **Loyola Marymount University,** Los Angeles, CA 90045, (213) 642-2854, 2842. Priv, MA, 4,000 stud, int fund. Number yrs: c. Comps: a, b, c, d, e, f, g, k. Curr elem: b, c.

Philip Woodard, **National University,** 3580 Aero Ct, San Diego, 92123, (619) 563-2672. Priv, MA, 12,000 stud, int fund. Number yrs: b. Comps: b, c, f, h, k. Curr elem: b.

Stephen McDonald, **Palomar College**, San Marcos, CA 92069, (619) 744-1150 x2399. Pub, cc, 18,734 stud, int fund. Number yrs: b. Comps: b, c, f, g, h, i.

Joseph Sierra, **Pasadena City College**, 1570 E Colorado Blvd, Pasadena, CA 91106, (818) 578-7371. Pub, cc, 14,000 stud, ext (NEH) & int fund. Number yrs: c. Comps: i, j. Curr elem: a.

Mary Meziere, **Pierce College**, Woodland Hills, CA 91371, (818) 347-0551. Pub, cc, 20,000 stud, int fund. Number yrs: a. Comps: b, e, h, k.

Judson Emerick, Art Dept, **Pomona College**, Claremont, CA 91711, (714) 621-8000 x2687. Priv, 4 yr, 1,400 stud, int fund. Number yrs: c. Comps: f, j. Curr elem: b.

Ann Johns, Acad Skills Ctr, **San Diego State University**, San Diego, CA 92182, (619) 265-5477. Pub, MA, 32,000 stud, ext (Chancellor, CSU system) and & int fund. Comps: a, b, c, d, e, f, i, j. Curr elem: a, c, d.

Jan Gregory, English, **San Francisco State University**, 1600 Holloway, San Francisco, CA 94132, (415) 338-7702. Pub, MA, 26,000 stud, ext fund (st lottery). Number yrs: a. Comps: a, d, g.

Sister Hilary Yoggerst, English, **St. John's Seminary College**, 5118 E Seminary Road, Camarillo, CA 93010, (805) 482-4697. Priv, 4 yr, 86 stud, int fund. Number yrs: b. Comps: b, c, e, h, j, k. Curr elem: a, d.

Carol Beran, English, **St. Mary's College of California**, Moraga, CA 94575, (415) 376-4411 x432. Priv, 4 yr, 1,600 stud, int fund. Number yrs: a. Comps: b, c, e, f, k.

Mary Ann Aschauer, English, **Santa Clara University**, Santa Clara, CA 95053, (408) 554-4308. Priv, MA, 3,200 stud, ext (NEH) & int fund. Number yrs: c. Comps: a, c, g, i, j, l. Curr elem: b.

Ellen R. Woods, **Stanford University**, Building One, Dean's Office, H & S, Stanford, CA 94305, (415) 723-9378. Priv, PhD, 13,200 stud, ext (donor gift) & int fund. Number yrs: c. Comps: a, d, g, j. Curr elem: c.

Jan Stanbrough, Campus Writing Ctr, **University of California, Davis**, CA 95616, (916) 752-8024. Pub, PhD, 20,847 stud, int fund. Comps: g, i, j. Curr elem: d.

Ellen Strenski, UCLA Writing Prog, 371 Kinsey Hall, **University of California, Los Angeles**, CA 90024-1384, (213) 825-8852. Pub, PhD, 32,000 stud, int fund. Number yrs: e. Comps: b, c, d, e, i, j, k. Curr elem: a, b, d.

Susan Peck MacDonald, Third College Writing Prog, D-009D, **University of California, San Diego**, La Jolla, CA 92093-0509, (619) 534-2742. Pub, PhD, int fund. Number yrs: c. Comps: c, d. Curr elem: b, d.

Muriel Zimmerman, Interdisc Writing Prog, Arts 1235, **University of California, Santa Barbara**, CA 93106, (805) 961-2462. Pub, PhD, 18,000 stud, int fund. Number yrs: c. Curr elem: b, d.

Virginia Draper, Coord, WAC, Stevenson College, **University of California, Santa Cruz**, CA 95064, (408) 429-2827. Pub, PhD, 8,400 stud, int fund. Comps: b, c, d, e, h, k, l. Curr elem: a, b, c.

Nancy Carrick, **University of Redlands**, PO Box 3080, Redlands, CA 92373-0999, (714) 793-2121 x4348, x4340. Priv, 4 yr, 1,200 stud, int fund. Number yrs: c. Comps: a, b, c, e, f, g, k. Curr elem: a, c.

Phyllis Kahaney, English, **University of San Diego**, Alcala Park, San Diego, CA 92110, (619) 260-4600 x4932. Priv, MA, 5,660 stud, ext (CAPHE) & int fund. Number yrs: c. Comps: a, c, e, i, j, k, l. Curr elem: a, b, c, d.

Michael McBride, Pol Science, **Whittier College**, Whittier, CA 90608, (213) 693-0771. Priv, 4 yr, 1,000 stud, ext (CAPHE) & int fund. Number yrs: b. Comps: a, b, c, d, e, f, i, j, k. Curr elem: a, b, c.

Colorado

Ruth Barton, **Colorado College**, Colorado Springs, CO 80903, (303) 473-2233 x2503. Priv, 4 yr, 1,850 stud, int fund. Number yrs: e. Comps: a, b, c, e, f, i, j, k, l. Curr elem: b, c, e.

Barbara M. Olds, Hum & Soc Sciences, **Colorado School of Mines**, Golden, CO 80228, (303) 273-3944, 3750. Pub, PhD, 2,000 stud, ext (Exxon Fdn) & int fund. Comps: a, c, k, l.

Jean Wyrick, Director of Comp, **Colorado State University**, Fort Collins, CO 80523, (303) 491-6428. Pub, PhD, int fund, number yrs: e. Comps: k.

James G. Erickson, **Fort Lewis College**, Durango, CO 81301, (303) 247-7454. Pub, 4 yr, 3,700 stud, int fund. Number yrs: e. Comps: b, g, i, k. Curr elem: a.

Penny Jackman, **Pikes Peak Community College**, 5675 S Academy Blvd, Colorado Springs, CO 80906, (303) 576-7711. Pub, cc, 10,000 stud, int fund. Number yrs: a. Comps: a, j.

Lt. Col. Perry D. Luckett, Asst. Dean of Faculty, **U.S. Air Force Academy/ DFA**, Colorado Springs, CO 80840, (303) 472-4195. Pub, 4 yr, 4,400 stud, int fund. Number yrs: a. Comps: b, c, e, j, k, l. Curr elem: b, c.

Janice N. Hays, Director of Comp, **University of Colorado**, Austin Bluffs Parkway, PO Box 7150, Colorado Springs, CO 80933-7150, (719) 593-3188. Pub, MA, 5,546 stud, ext (NEH) & int fund. Number yrs: d. Comps: b, e, k, l. Curr elem: b, c.

Connecticut

L. Ress, Writing Center Director, **Fairfield University**, N. Benson Rd., Fairfield, CT 06430, (203) 254-4000 x2214. Priv, MA, 5,000 stud, int fund. Number yrs: d. Comps: a, e, i, k.

Peter Ulisse, **Housatonic Community College**, 510 Barnum Avenue, Bridgeport, CT 06608, (203) 579-6441. Pub, cc, 2,200 stud, ext fund (Title III). Number yrs: a. Comps: b, c, e, f, j. Curr elem: a, d.

Kathleen Sullivan, **Manchester Community College**, Box 1046, Manchester, CT 06040 (203) 647-6264. Pub, cc, 6,000 stud, int fund. Number yrs: a. Comps: b, c, f, j, k. Curr elem: a, d.

Arnold H. Chadderton, **Post College**, Country Club Road, Waterbury, CT 06708, (203) 755-0121 x269. Priv, 4 yr, 1,200 stud, int fund. Number yrs: c. Comp: k.

J. David Hankins, English, **University of Connecticut**, Storrs, CT 06250, (203) 486-2321. Pub, PhD, 15,000 stud. Curr elem: b, c.

William L. Stull, English, **University of Hartford**, West Hartford, CT 06117, (203) 243-4138. Priv, 4 yr, 3,500 stud, ext fund (Mellon Fdn). Number yrs: b. Comps: a, c, e, g, k. Curr elem: a, b, c.

Leslie E. Moore, Linda H. Peterson, Stuart Moulthrop; English, **Yale University**, PO Box 3545, New Haven, CT 06520, (203) 432-2233. Priv, PhD, 5,100 stud, ext fund (Pew Memorial Trust). Comps: d, i. Curr elem: a, b, c, d.

Delaware

George Miller, English, **University of Delaware**, Newark, DE 19716, (302) 451-2363. Pub, PhD, 14,000 stud. Number yrs: c. Comps: a, b, c, d, e, h, j, k, l. Curr elem: b, c.

District of Columbia

Russell C. Olson, Govt Dept, **Gallaudet University**, Washington, DC, 20002, (202) 651-5547. Pub, 4 yr, 7,000 stud, int fund. Comps: a, c, e, g, i, k. Curr elem: c, d.

James F. Slevin, English, **Georgetown University**, Washington, DC 20057, (202) 687-7565. Priv, PhD, 11,000 stud, ext (NEH) & int fund. Number yrs: d. Comps: a, c, d, e, g, h, i, k. Curr elem: b, c, d.

Miriam Dow and Kim Moreland, English, **George Washington University**, Washington, DC 20052, (202) 994-6180. Priv, PhD, 3,500 stud (Arts & Sciences), int fund. Number yrs: b. Comps: a, c. Curr elem: c.

Florida

Anne M. Marcus, **Edison Community College**, Fort Myers, FL 33906, (813) 489-9331. Pub, cc, 6,000 stud, int fund. Number yrs: c. Comps: a, b, j. Curr elem: c.

Joan Carver, Dean, Arts & Sciences, **Jacksonville University**, Jacksonville, FL 32211, (904) 744-3950. Priv, 4 yr, 2,100 stud, int fund. Number yrs: c. Comps: b, c, f, g, i, k. Curr elem: b, c.

James Preston, English, South, **Miami-Dade Community College**, 11011 SW 104 Street, Miami, FL 33176, (305) 347-2522. Pub, cc, int fund. Number yrs: d.

Dion K. Brown, **Polk Community College**, Winter Haven, FL 33881, (813) 397-1037. Pub, cc, 5,000 stud, int fund. Number yrs: c. Comps: b, c, g, i, j, k. Curr elem: a.

Twila Yates Papay, Director of Writing Prog, **Rollins College**, Box 2655, Winter Park, FL 32789, (305) 646-2191, 2308. Priv, 4 yr, 1,400 stud, ext (Lilly, NEH) & int fund. Number yrs: e. Comps: a, b, c, g, i, j, k, l. Curr elem: b, c.

Samuel L. Cunningham, **Tallahassee Community College**, Tallahassee, FL 32304, (904) 576-5181. Pub, cc, 7,200 stud, ext fund (state). Number yrs: b. Comps: b, c, d, f, g, j, k. Curr elem: b, c.

Ronald Newman, English, **University of Miami**, PO Box 8145, Coral Gables, FL 33124, (305) 284-3090. Priv, PhD, 13,345 stud, int fund. Number yrs: a. Comps: k. Curr elem: b, c.

Georgia

James L. Hill, English & Mod Lang, **Albany State College**, Albany, GA 31705, (912) 430-4833. Pub, 4 yr, 2,005 stud, ext fund (Exxon Fdn). Comps: b, g, j, k, l.

Richard Nordquist, Director of Writing Ctr, **Armstrong State College**, 11935 Abercorn Street, Savannah, GA 31419, (912) 927-5210. Pub, 4 yr, 3,000 stud, int fund. Number yrs: c. Comps: b, c, e, g, h, i, j, k, l. Curr elem: d.

Barbara Bird, **Atlanta Junior College**, 1630 Stewart Avenue, Atlanta, GA 30310, (404) 656-6363. Pub, cc, 1,400 stud, ext fund (Title III). Number yrs: b. Comps: b, c, e, g, i, j, k.

Harry Rusche, English, and Rosemary Magee, Assoc. Dean of the College, **Emory University**, Atlanta, GA 30322, (404) 727-6426, 0765. Priv, PhD, 4,000 stud, ext (Ford Fdn) & int fund. Number yrs: b. Comps: a, b, c, d, e, g, i, j. Curr elem: a, c.

Gregory G. Colomb, English, **Georgia Institute of Technology**, Atlanta, GA 30332, (404) 894-2737. Pub, PhD, 1,100 stud, ext (local fdn) & int fund. Number yrs: a. Comps: a, b, c, d, e, l. Curr elem: b, c.

Sandra L. Gallemore, Phys Educ, LB8073-01, **Georgia Southern College**, Statesboro, GA 30460, (912) 618-5266. Pub, MA, 8,750 stud, ext & int fund. Number yrs: d. Comps: b, f, h, i, j, k.

Brenda W. Thomas, **La Grange College**, La Grange, GA 30240, (404) 882-2911 x256. Priv, 4 yr, 911 stud, int fund. Number yrs: b. Comps: b, c, d, e, j, k. Curr elem: a, b.

Marjorie T. Davis, Assoc. Provost, **Mercer University**, Macon, GA 31207, (912) 744-4003. Priv, MA, 2,200 stud, ext (Title III) & int fund. Comps: a, b, c, f, h, i, j, k. Curr elem: c.

Robert C. Wess, **Southern College of Technology**, Marietta, GA 30060, (404) 424-7202. Pub, 4 yr, 3,600 stud, int fund. Comps: b, c, f, g, h, j, k, l. Curr elem: c.

Jacqueline Jones Royster, **Spelman College**, Box 850, 350 Spelman Lane SW, Atlanta, GA 30314, (404) 681-3643 x362. Ext (Title III, SEF, Quill, FIPSE) & int fund. Number yrs: e. Comps: a, b, c, e, f, g, h, i, j, k, l. Curr elem: c.

Thomas E. Dasher, English, **Valdosta State College**, Valdosta, GA 31698, (912) 333-7078. Pub, MA, 7,056 stud, int fund. Number yrs: b. Comps: b, c, g, j, k. Curr elem: b.

Hawaii

Carol K. Bass, Lang Arts, **Leeward Community College**, Pearl City, HI 96782, (808) 455-0429, 0330. Pub, cc, 5,800 stud, int fund. Number yrs: a. Comps: b, g, j.

Sandra Hammond, Gen'l Ed Div, **University of Hawaii at Hilo**, Hilo, HI 96720, (808) 961-9452. Pub, 4 yr, 3,500 stud, int fund. Number yrs: a. Comps: e, h.

Henry B. Chapin, **University of Hawaii—West Oahu College**, 96-043 Ala-Ike, Pearl City, HI 96782, (808) 456-5921. 2 yr upper div, 500 stud, int fund. Number yrs: b. Comps: a, b, c, e, f, j. Curr elem: c.

Idaho

Roy F. Fox, English, **Boise State University**, Boise, ID 83725, (208) 385-1824, 1246. Pub, MA, 11,000 stud, ext (NEH) & int fund. Comps: a, b, c, d, e, h, j, k. Curr elem: a, b, c.

Susan H. Swetnam, **Idaho State University**, Box 8216, Pocatello, ID 83209, (208) 236-2893. Pub, MA, 7,000 stud, int fund. Comps: f, k. Curr elem: b.

Illinois

Karin Youngberg, English, **Augustana College**, Rock Island, IL 61201, (309) 794-7379. Priv, 4 yr, 2,100 stud, ext & int fund. Number yrs: e. Comps: a, b, c, d, e, i, j, k, l. Curr elem: c.

Ann Barnard, English, **Blackburn College**, Carlinville, IL 62626, (217) 3231 x314. Priv, 4 yr, 500 stud, ext fund (Lilly Fdn). Number yrs: a. Comps: b, c, j, k. Curr elem: c.

Judith Rosenberg, Assoc. Dean, Comm Arts, **College of Lake County**, Grayslake, IL 60030, (312) 223-6601 x550. Pub, cc, 12,770 stud, int fund. Number yrs: c. Comps: a, c, d, e, j, k. Curr elem: d.

Philip J. Klukoff and Jeff Schiff, **Columbia College**, 600 S Michigan Ave, Chicago, IL 60605, (312) 663-1600 x73-251, 73-252. Priv, 4 yr, 5,700 stud, ext (Lilly Fdn) & int fund. Number yrs: a. Comps: a, b, g, j, k. Curr elem: a, b, c.

Patricia Y. Murray, English, **DePaul University**, 802 W Belden Ave, Chicago, IL 60614, (312) 341-8622. Priv, MA, 13,000 stud, ext (NEH) & int fund. Comps: b, c. Curr elem: a.

Robert W. Swords, English, **Elmhurst College**, Elmhurst, IL 60126. Int fund. Number yrs: a. Comps: a, b.

J. Plett, **Greenville College**, Greenville, IL 62246. Priv, 4 yr, ext fund (Christian College Consortium). Number yrs: b. Comps: a, b, d, e, j, k. Curr elem: a.

Mary Cignarelli, English, **Illinois Central College**, East Peoria, IL 61635, (309) 694-5352. Pub, cc, 13,000 stud, int fund. Comps: b, c, e, g, h, k. Curr elem: a.

Douglas D. Hesse, English, **Illinois State University**, Normal, IL 61761, (309) 438-7349. Pub, MA, 22,000 stud, ext fund (state). Number yrs: c. Comps: a, b, c, d, e, k. Curr elem: c.

Barbara Bowman, English, **Illinois Wesleyan University**, Bloomington, IL 61702, (309) 556-3245. Priv, 4 yr, 1,650 stud, ext (Lilly Fdn) & int fund. Number yrs: e. Comps: a, b, c, d, e, g, k. Curr elem: a, b, c, d.

John S. Shea, Director of WAC, **Loyola University**, Damen 205, Chicago, IL 60626, (312) 508-2240. Priv, PhD, 3,800 stud, int fund. Number yrs: b. Comps: b, c, g, k. Curr elem: d.

Terry Shepherd, English, **Millikin University**, 1184 W Main, Decatur, IL 62522, (217) 424-6280. Priv, 4 yr, 1,500 stud, int fund. Number yrs: b. Comps: a, g, j, k.

Gary D. Willcharst, English, **Monmouth College**, Monmouth, IL 61462, (309) 457-2377. Priv, 4 yr, 670 stud, int fund. Number yrs: a. Comps: a, c, e, k. Curr elem: b.

Mary Lu Fennell, **Principia College**, Elsah, IL 62028, (618) 374-2131 x212. Priv, 4 yr, 700 stud, int fund. Number yrs: e. Comps: b, c, e, g, i, j, k. Curr elem: d.

James P. Flynn, **Thornton Community College**, 15800 S State St, South Holland, IL 60473, (312) 596-2000. Priv, cc, int fund. Number yrs: a. Comps: b, c, j.

Joe Williams, English, **University of Chicago**, Chicago, IL 60637, (312) 702-7997. Priv, PhD, 6,700 stud, ext (fdns) & int fund. Comps: a, b, d, e, f, i, k. Curr elem: b, d.

David A. Jolliffe, English, **University of Illinois**, PO Box 4348, Chicago, IL 60680, (312) 413-2249. Int fund. Number yrs: a. Comps: k, l. Curr elem: c, d.

Bruce H. Leland, English, **Western Illinois University**, Macomb, IL 61455, (309) 298-2136. Pub, MA, 10,000 stud. Number yrs: a. Comps: b. Curr elem: b.

Sharon Coolidge, English, **Wheaton College**, Wheaton, IL 60187, (312) 260-3782. Priv, 4 yr, 2,100 stud, ext fund (Pew Memorial Trust, Glenmede Trust). Number yrs: b. Comps: a, c, e, g, j, k, l. Curr elem: c.

Rocco Blasi, **Wright College**, 3400 N Austin Ave, Chicago, IL 60634, (312) 794-3160. Pub, cc, 5,450 stud. Number yrs: b. Comps: b, c, i, l. Curr elem: a, b, c, d.

Indiana

Lynn E. Kloesel, English, **Butler University**, 4600 Sunset Ave, Indianapolis, IN 46208, (317) 283-9223. Priv, MA, 3,000 stud, ext fund (Lilly Endowment). Number yrs: b. Comps: a, c, i, j.

John White, Assoc. V-P for Acad Affairs; Cynthia Cornell & Robert Newton, Assoc. Coords for Faculty Dev, Writing Prog, **DePauw University**, Greencastle, IN 46135, (317) 658-4739, 4676, 4715. Priv, 4 yr, 2,300 stud, ext (Lilly Fdn) & int fund. Comps: a, d, e, g, h, i, j, k.

Barbara L. Cambridge, **Indiana University-Purdue University at Indianapolis**, 425 Agnes, Indianapolis, IN 46202, (317) 274-3824. Int fund. Number yrs: b. Comps: e. Curr elem: b.

Gary Phillips, Lead Writing Inst, **Indiana Vocational and Technical College**, One West 26th, Indianapolis, IN 46208, (317) 921-4929. Int fund. Number yrs: a.

Susan Winger, **Taylor University**, Upland, IN 46989, (317) 998-7106. Priv, 4 yr, 1,500 stud, ext (Pew Fdn) & int fund. Comps: a, b, e, f, g, j, k, l. Curr elem: a, b, c, d.

Edward Kline, Freshman Writing Prog, **University of Notre Dame**, Notre Dame, IN 46556, (219) 239-5578. Priv, PhD, 10,000 stud, int fund. Number yrs: e. Comps: a, b, e, h, i. Curr elem: a, d.

Iowa

Cindy Nahrwold, Writing Lab Director, **Briar Cliff College**, 3303 Rebecca St, Sioux City, IA 51104, (712) 279-5462. Priv, 4 yr, 1,000 stud, ext (Title III) & int fund. Comps: b, c, e, g, j, k. Curr elem: a, c.

Mathilda Liberman, **Grinnell College**, Grinnell, IA 50112, (515) 269-3117. Int fund. Number yrs: e. Comps: a, k. Curr elem: c.

Marty S. Knepper, English, **Morningside College**, Sioux City, IA 51106, (712) 274-5264. Priv, 4 yr, 2,000 stud, int fund. Number yrs: c. Comps: a, c, e, f, g, h, i, j, k.

Charlene Eblen, English, **University of Northern Iowa**, Cedar Falls, IA 50614, (319) 273-3805. Pub, MA, 11,000 stud, int fund. Comps: a, c, e, f, h, i, k. Curr elem: a, c.

Kansas

Marvin Bahr, **Barton County Community College**, R. R. 3, Great Bend, KS 67530-9283, (316) 792-2701. Pub, cc, 1,900 stud, int fund. Number yrs: a. Comps: a, c, g, j. Curr elem: a, c.

Jack Holligen, **Johnson County Community College**, 12345 College Blvd, Overland Park, KS 66210, (913) 469-8500 x3610. Pub, cc, 10,000 stud, int fund. Comps: b, e, g, j, k.

Robert D. Stein, English, **Washburn University**, Topeka, KS 66621, (913) 295-6441. Pub, 4 yr, 6,000 stud, int fund. Number yrs: c. Comps: a, b, e, k. Curr elem: b.

Kentucky

William Schafer, **Berea College**, CPO 1868, Berea, KY 40404, (606) 986-9341 x6448. Priv, 4 yr, 1,650 stud. Number yrs: e. Comps: a, b, i, j, k. Curr elem: a, b, c.

Charles F. Whitaker, **Eastern Kentucky University**, Wallace 217, Richmond, KY 40475, (606) 622-2093. Pub, MA, 13,000 stud, int fund. Number yrs: a. Comps: b, c, i. Curr elem: a, b.

Bob Darrell, English & Journalism, **Kentucky Wesleyan College**, Box 64, Owensboro, KY 42302-1039, (502) 926-3111 x271, 270. Priv, 800 stud. Number yrs: b. Comps: e, k. Curr elem: a, c.

Stephen R. Thomas, **Maysville Community College**, Maysville, KY 41056, (606) 759-5141. Pub, cc, 780 stud. Number yrs: a. Comps: b, e, g, j, k. Curr elem: a.

Christine Cetrulo, Linda Combes, Jan Isenhour, **University of Kentucky**, 1215 Patterson Office Tower, Lexington, KY 40506-0027, (606) 257-1115. Pub, PhD, 22,100 stud, int fund. Comps: a, b, c, d, j, k. Curr elem: d.

Joseph Comprone, English, **University of Louisville**, Louisville, KY 40292, (502) 588-6896. Pub, PhD, 20,000 stud, int fund. Number yrs: c. Comps: a, b, d, f, j, l. Curr elem: a, b, c.

Karen L. Pelz, English, **Western Kentucky University**, Cherry Hall 135, Bowling Green, KY 42101, (502) 745-5712. Pub, MA, 13,500 stud, int fund. Number yrs: c. Comps: a, b, c, e, g, h, j, k. Curr elem: d.

Louisiana

Helen R. Malin, **Dillard University**, New Orleans, LA 70122. Priv, 4 yr, 1,320 stud, ext (CAPHE, UNCF) & int fund. Comps: b, c. Curr elem: a, c, d.

Kate Adams, WAC Prog, **Loyola University**, New Orleans, LA 70121, (504) 865-2297. Priv, 4 yr, 5,000 stud, ext (Schlieder Ed Fdn) & int fund. Number yrs: b. Comps: b, c, e, g, i, k.

Argiro L. Morgan, **Xavier University of Louisiana**, PO Box 32A, New Orleans, LA 70125, (504) 483-7619. Priv, MA, 2,200 stud, ext fund (Bush-Hewlett). Number yrs: b. Comps: a, c, e, h, j, k. Curr elem: a, b.

Maine

Jean Sanborn, English; Jane Hunter, History, **Colby College**, Waterville, ME 04901, (207) 872-3281. Priv, 4 yr, 1,700 stud, int fund. Number yrs: c. Comps: b, c, e, g, i, j, k.

Susan K. Loomis, **Maine Maritime Academy**, Castine, ME 04421, (207) 325-4311 x344. Pub, MA, 550 stud, int fund. Number yrs: a. Comps: a, f, h. Curr elem: a, c.

A. Bruce Dean, English, **University of Maine, Farmington**, ME 04938, (207) 778-3501. Pub, 4 yr, 2,300 stud, int fund. Number yrs: e. Comps: b, c, f, g, h, i, j, l. Curr elem: b, c.

Harvey Kail, English, **University of Maine, Orono**, ME 04473, (207) 581-3829. Pub, PhD, 11,000 stud, int fund. Number yrs: a. Comps: a, b, c, e, g, j, k. Curr elem: a, b, c.

Maryland

Shirley Rompf, English, **Catonsville Community College**, 800 S Rolling Rd, Catonsville, MD 21228, (301) 455-4377. Pub, cc, 11,000 stud, int fund. Comps: e, g.

Gail Bounds, **Chesapeake College**, PO Box 8, Wye Mills, MD 21679, (301) 822-5400 x331. Pub, cc, 3,000 stud, int fund. Number yrs: b. Comps: b, c, f, g, h, i, k.

Al Starr, English, **Essex Community College**, Baltimore, MD 21237, (301) 522-1623. Pub, cc, 10,000 stud, int fund. Number yrs: d. Comps: b, g, j, k.

Phyllis R. Hamilton, Letters, **Frederick Community College**, Frederick, MD 21701, (301) 694-5240. Pub, cc, 3,500 stud, int fund. Number yrs: a. Comps: b, k, l.

Dennis Gartner, English, **Frostburg State University**, Frostburg, MD 21532, (301) 689-4221. Pub, MA, 4,200 stud. Number yrs: b. Comps: b, k. Curr elem: a, b.

Hagerstown Junior College, 751 Robinwood Dr, Hagerstown, MD 21740. Pub, cc, 2,800 stud. Number yrs: a. Comp: k.

Carl Henderson, **Harford Community College**, 401 Thomas Run Rd, Bel Air, MD 21014, (301) 836-4300. Pub, cc, 4,500 stud, int fund. Number yrs: c. Comps: b, d, e, j, k.

Barbara C. Mallonee, Dept of Writing, **Loyola College**, 4501 N Charles St, Baltimore, MD 21210, (301) 323-1010. Priv, 4 yr, 2,500 stud, ext (NEH) & int fund. Number yrs: d. Comps: a, b, f, h, l. Curr elem: a.

Barbara Stout, **Montgomery College**, Rockville, MD 20850, (301) 279-5150. Pub, cc, 19,000 stud, int fund. Number yrs: c. Comps: b, g, h, i, j, k.

Joyce N. Magnotto, WAC Director, **Prince Georges Community College**, Largo, MD 20772-2199, (301) 322-0582. Pub, cc, 23,000 stud, int fund. Number yrs: d. Comps: a, b, d, e, g, h, i, j, k. Curr elem: d.

Connie White, English, **Salisbury State College**, Salisbury, MD 21801, (301) 543-6444. Pub, 4 yr, 4,900 stud, int fund. Number yrs: d. Comps: b, f, k. Curr elem: a.

Thomas J. Slaker, Dean, **St. John's College**, Annapolis, MD 21404, (301) 263-2371. Priv, 4 yr, 400 stud, int fund. Number yrs: e. Comps: g.

H. Fil Dowling, Jr, English, **Towson State University**, Baltimore, MD 21204, (301) 321-2864. Pub, MA, 10,000 stud, int fund. Number yrs: e. Comps: a, b, e, f, j, k, l. Curr elem: c.

Carol Burke, English, **U.S. Naval Academy**, Annapolis, MD 21402. Pub, 4 yr, 3,500 stud, int fund. Number yrs: c. Comps: a, c, e, j, k, l.

Carol Fitzpatrick, English, **University of Maryland-Baltimore County**, Catonsville, MD 21228, (301) 455-3286, 3284. Pub, PhD, 9,200 stud, int fund. Number yrs: c. Comps: b, c, d, j, k. Curr elem: a, b, d.

Nancy Shapiro, Jr Writing Prog, English, **University of Maryland, College Park**, MD 20742, (301) 454-4163. Pub, PhD, 30,000 stud, int fund. Number yrs: d. Comps: a, b, c, h, i, j, k, l. Curr elem: b.

Massachusetts

Angela G. Dorenkamp, **Assumption College**, 500 Salisbury, Worcester, MA 01609-1296. Priv, 4 yr, 1,700 stud, int fund. Number yrs: d. Comps: b, e, f, h, j, k. Curr elem: c.

Linda Micheli, **Bentley College**, G93, Waltham, MA 02254, MA, 4,000 stud, int fund. Number yrs: c. Comps: b, h, j, l. Curr elem: a.

John Burr, English, **Brandeis University**, Rabb 144, Waltham, MA 02254-9110. Priv, PhD, 3,000 stud, int fund. Number yrs: b. Comps: b, c, d, f, i, j, k. Curr elem: c, d.

Leone C. Scanlon, Director of the Writing Ctr, **Clark University**, 950 Main St, Worcester, MA 01610, (617) 793-7469. Int fund. Number yrs: e. Comps: a, c, d, e, i, k. Curr elem: a, c.

Patricia Bizzell, English, **College of the Holy Cross**, Worcester, MA 01610, (617) 793-2524. Priv, 4 yr, 2,500 stud, ext (Hewlett-Mellon Fdn) & int fund. Number yrs: d. Comps: a, b, c, d, e, h, j, k. Curr elem: a, b, c.

Terry Grahar, **Fitchburg State College**, Fitchburg, MA 01420, (617) 345-2151 x3267. Pub, MA, 3,000 stud, int fund. Number yrs: c. Comps: b, c, f, g, j, k.

Sue Lonoff, Expository Writing Prog, **Harvard University**, 3rd Fl Union, Cambridge, MA 02138, (617) 492-3659. Priv, PhD, 5,000 stud, int fund. Number yrs: b. Comps: a, b, d, e. Curr elem: a.

Rosalind Williams, **Massachusetts Institute of Technology**, Cambridge, MA 02139, (617) 253-7894. Priv, PhD, 4,000 stud, int fund. Number yrs: e. Comps: d.

Marion Bailey, **North Shore Community College**, 300 Broad St, Lynn, MA 01907, (922) NSCC x259. Pub, cc, 2,000 stud, int fund. Number yrs: c. Comps: b, c, e, j, k.

Hannah Laipson, English, **Quinsigamond Community College**, 670 W Boylston St, Worcester, MA 01606, (617) 853-2300. Pub, cc, 2,000 stud, int fund. Number yrs: b. Comps: b, c, e, g, h, j, k.

Lowry Pei, English, **Simmons College**, 300 The Fenway, Boston, MA 02115, (617) 738-2143. Priv, 4 yr, 1,600 stud, int fund. Number yrs: b. Comps: b, c, e, f, h, j, k. Curr elem: c.

Jamie Hutchinson, Natalie Harper, Pat Sharpe, English, **Simon's Rock of Bard College**, Great Barrington, MA 01230, (413) 528-0771. Priv, 4 yr, 300 stud, int fund. Number yrs: c. Comps: a, k, l. Curr elem: a.

Virginia G. Polanski, **Stonehill College,** North Easton, MA 02356. Priv, 4 yr, 1,600 stud, int fund. Number yrs: e. Comps: b, c, d, e, f, h, j, k, l. Curr elem: a.

Bette Mandl, English, **Suffolk University**, Beacon Hill, Boston, MA 02114, (617) 573-8274. Priv, 4 yr, 2,000 stud, int fund. Number yrs: d. Comps: b, c, f, g, j, k.

Ann J. Van Sant, English, **Tufts University**, 207 E Hall, Medford, MA 02155, (617) 628-5000 x2461. Priv, PhD, 4,800 stud, int fund. Number yrs: a. Comps: a, c, i, j. Curr elem: c.

Charles Moran, Writing Prog, **University of Massachusetts, Amherst**, Bartlett Hall 305, Amherst, MA 01003, (413) 545-0610. Pub, PhD, 27,000 stud, int fund. Number yrs: c. Comps: b, f, i, k. Curr elem: c.

Louise Z. Smith, English, **University of Massachusetts, Boston**, MA 02125, (617) 929-8300. Pub, MA, 13,000 stud, ext (Ford Fdn) & int fund. Number yrs: e. Comps: b, e, g, k. Curr elem: c.

Marcia Stubbs, Coord of Writing Prog, **Wellesley College**, Wellesley, MA 02181, (617) 235-0320 x2576. Priv, 4 yr, 2,257 stud, ext (gifts) & int fund. Number yrs: c. Comps: b, c, e, i, j, k. Curr elem: a, b.

Ann St. Germain, **Wentworth Institute of Technology**, Boston, MA 02115, (617) 442-9010 x370. Priv, 4 yr, 3,000 stud, int fund. Number yrs: b. Comps: b, e, g, k.

Beverly Clark, **Wheaton College**, Norton, MA 02766, (617) 285-7722 x491. Priv, 4 yr, 1,110 stud, ext (FIPSE) and int fund. Number yrs: e. Comps: a, b, c, e, f, k. Curr elem: a, c, d.

Peter D. Grudin, **Williams College**, Williamstown, MA 01267, (413) 597-2520. Priv, 4 yr, 2,000 stud, int fund. Number yrs: c. Comps: b, c, d, k.

Michigan

Douglas Jones, English, **Andrews University**, Berrien Springs, MI 49104, (616) 471-3171. Priv, PhD, 2,783 stud, int fund. Number yrs: d. Comps: b, k. Curr elem: b.

Rick Amidon, **Baker College**, Flint, MI 48507, (517) 723-5251. Priv, 4 yr, 810 stud, int fund. Number yrs: c. Comps: a, b, c, e, f, g, k. Curr elem: d.

John Alexander, Lang & Lit, **Ferris State University**, Big Rapids, MI 49307, (616) 592-2519. Int fund. Number yrs: e. Comps: b, c, e, g, j, k, l. Curr elem: b, c, d.

Janice Balyeat, **Grand Rapids Junior College**, 143 Bostwick NE, Grand Rapids, MI 49503, (616) 456-4869. Pub, cc, 10,000 stud, int fund. Number yrs: a. Comps: e, g.

Benjamin G. Lockerd, Jr, English, **Grand Valley State College**, Allendale, MI 49401, (616) 895-3588. Pub, 4 yr, 8,000 stud, int fund. Number yrs: e. Comps: b, c, e, f, j, k. Curr elem: c, d.

Robert H. Bentley, Comm, **Lansing Community College**, Lansing, MI 48901-7210, (517) 483-1040. Pub, cc, 21,000 stud. Number yrs: a. Comps: g, j.

Dennis Thompson, **Macomb County Community College**, 14500 Twelve Mile Rd, Warren, MI 48093-3896. Pub, cc, 28,000 stud, int fund. Number yrs: b. Comps: a, b, c, e, h, l. Curr elem: d.

Stephen Tchudi, Ctr for Literacy and Learning, **Michigan State University**, East Lansing, MI 48824, (517) 355-7570. Pub, PhD, 43,000 stud, int fund. Number yrs: a. Comps: a, b, f, i, j, l. Curr elem: a, b, c.

Elizabeth A. Flynn, Humanities, **Michigan Technological University**, Houghton, MI 49931, (906) 487-2007. Pub, PhD, 6,100 stud, ext (General Motors Fdn) & int fund. Number yrs: e. Comps: a, c, j, k, l.

John M. Holladay, **Monroe County Community College**, Monroe, MI 48161, (313) 242-7300 x340. Pub, cc, 3,200 stud, int fund. Number yrs: a. Comps: a, b, g, j, k, l.

Robert T. Plec, **Oakland Community College**, 2900 Featherstone Rd, Auburn Hills, MI 48057, (313) 853-4288. Pub, cc, 25,000 stud, int fund. Number yrs: a. Comps: a, b, c, g, h, j.

Deborah Keller-Cohen, Director, English Comp Board, **University of Michigan**, 1025 Angell Hall, Ann Arbor, MI 48109, (313) 764-0429. Pub, PhD, 17,300 stud, int fund. Number yrs: e. Comps: b, d, k, l. Curr elem: c.

Barbara Couture, Director of Comp, English, **Wayne State University**, Detroit, MI 48202, (313) 577-7696. Pub, PhD, 29,000 stud. Number yrs: a. Comps: a, e, g, j, k, l. Curr elem: a, c.

Lynne McCauley, **Western Michigan University**, 201 Moore, Kalamazoo, MI 49008 (618) 383-8062. Pub, PhD, 22,000 stud, int fund. Number yrs: e. Comps: a, b, c, d, e, f, g, h, j, k. Curr elem: a, c.

Minnesota

Terry Dilley, **Austin Community College**, 1600 8th Ave NW, Austin, MN 55912, (507) 433-0531. Pub, cc, 800 stud, ext fund (Bush Fdn). Number yrs: c. Comps: a, b, c, d, j, l.

Carol Avelsgaard, Math, **Bemidji State University**, 1500 Birchmont Dr NE, Bemidji, MN 56601, (218) 755-3987. Pub, 4 yr, 4,000 stud, ext fund (Bush Fdn). Number yrs: d. Comps: a, c, g.

Doug Hebbard, **Brainerd Community College**, Brainerd, MN 56401, (218) 828-2339. Ext fund (Bush Fdn). Number yrs: c. Comps: b, c, e, i, k.

Robert Tisdale and Elizabeth Cirrer, English, **Carleton College**, Northfield, MN 55057, (507) 663-4315, 4082. Priv, 4 yr, 1,800 stud, ext (NW Area Fdn) & int fund. Number yrs: e. Comps: a, b, c, d, e, j, k. Curr elem: a, d.

Michael Bellamy, English, **College of St. Thomas**, St. Paul, MN 55105, (612) 647-5306. Priv, 4 yr, 4,000 stud, ext (Bush Fdn) & int fund. Number yrs: c. Comps: a, c, e, i. Curr elem: c.

Arlen Koestler, **Dr. Martin Luther King College**, New Ulm, MN 56073, (507) 354-8221 x205. Priv, 4 yr, 485 stud, ext fund (AAL). Number yrs: c. Comps: a, c, f.

116

Margaret Kratzke, **Fergus Falls Community College**, 1411 Terrace Dr, Fergus Falls, MN 56537, (218) 739-7533. Pub, cc, 700 stud, ext (Bush Fdn) & int fund. Number yrs: c. Comps: a, b, c, i.

Gretchen Flesher, **Gustavus Adolphus College**, Box 1437, St. Peter, MN 56082, (507) 931-7392. Priv, 4 yr, 2,200 stud, ext (Bush Fdn) & int fund. Number yrs: c. Comps: b, e, f, j, k. Curr elem: a, c.

Alice Moorhead, **Hamline University**, St. Paul, MN 55104, (612) 641-2800. Priv, 4 yr, 1,300 stud, ext (donor gifts) & int fund. Number yrs: c. Comps: a, c, e, i, j, k. Curr elem: a, b, c.

Michael Keenan, English, **Macalester College**, St. Paul, MN 55105, (612) 696-6387, 6506. Priv, 4 yr, 1,300 stud, int fund. Number yrs: d. Comps: a, b, c, e, k. Curr elem: c.

Erik F. Storlie, **Minneapolis Community College**, 1501 Hennepin Ave, Minneapolis, MN 55403, (612) 341-7112. Ext fund. Number yrs: d. Comps: a, b, c, e, h, i, j, k, l. Curr elem: d.

Keith A. Tandy, **Moorhead State University**, Moorhead, MN 56560, (218) 236-4677. Pub, MA, 8,200 stud, ext (Bush Fdn) & int fund. Number yrs: e. Comps: b, c, f, i.

Delores A. Wade, **North Hennepin Community College**, 7411 85th Ave North, Brooklyn Park, MN 55445, (612) 424-0824. Pub, cc, 4,000 stud, ext fund (Bush Fdn). Number yrs: c. Comps: a, b, c, e, i, j, k. Curr elem: a.

Patricia J. Bartlett, **Rainy River Community College**, International Falls, MN 56649, (218) 285-7722 x221. Pub, cc, 650 stud, ext fund (Bush Fdn). Number yrs: c. Comps: a, b, c, e, g, i, j, k, l.

Richard Dillman, English, **St. Cloud State University**, St. Cloud, MN 56301. Pub, MA, 15,500 stud, ext (Bush Fdn, NEH) & int fund. Number yrs: e. Comps: a, b, c, e, g. Curr elem: d.

Nancy Hynes, **St. John's University**, Collegeville, MN 56321 and **College of St. Benedict**, St. Joseph, MN 56374, (612) 363-5995. Priv, 4 yr, 3,800 stud, ext (Bush Fdn, NW Area Fdn) & int fund. Number yrs: d. Comps: a, c, e, g, j, k. Curr elem: a, c, d.

Olivia Frey, English, **St. Olaf College**, Northfield, MN 55057, (507) 663-3201. Priv, 4 yr, 3,000 stud, int fund. Number yrs: e. Comps: a, b, c, e, i, j, k, l. Curr elem: b, c.

Lillian Bridwell-Bowles, Comp Prog, **University of Minnesota**, Minneapolis, MN 55455, (612) 625-2888. Pub, PhD, 48,000 stud, ext (Deluxe Check) & int fund. Number yrs: d. Comps: b, c, d, g, k. Curr elem: b, c, d.

Will Rawn, Arts & Sciences Div, **University of Minnesota Technical College at Crookston**, MN 56716, (218) 281-6510 x378. Pub, cc, 1,200 stud, int fund. Number yrs: b. Comps: a, e, k.

Mary E. Rieder, **Winona State University**, 407 Somsen Hall, Winona, MN 55987, (507) 457-5183. Pub, MA, 5,200 stud, ext fund (Bush Fdn). Number yrs: d. Comps: a, c, k.

Charles Moore, **Worthington Community College**, 1914 Summit Ave, Worthington, MN 56187, (507) 372-2107. Pub, cc, 700 stud, ext fund (Bush Fdn). Number yrs: c. Comps: a, b, g, i, j, k. Curr elem: d.

Mississippi

Jerry Dallas, History, **Delta State University**, Cleveland, MS 38733, (601) 846-4176. Pub, 4 yr, 3,500 stud, ext (Hardin Fdn) & int fund. Number yrs: c. Comps: a, b, c, f, g, j, k.

Marla L. Cowie, Coord, Spec Acad Proj, **Mississippi Valley State University,** Itta Bena, MS 38941, (601) 254-9041. Pub, 4 yr, 2,000 stud, ext (community donations) & int fund. Number yrs: b. Comps: f, l. Curr elem: c.

Benedict C. Njoku, Humanities, **Rust College,** 150 Rust Ave, Holly Springs, MS 38635-2328, (601) 252-4661. Priv, 4 yr, 919 stud, int fund. Number yrs: b. Comps: c, d, g, k. Curr elem: a, b, d.

David Roberts, **University of Southern Mississippi,** Hattiesburg, MS 39406-0021. Pub, PhD, 10,000 stud, ext (FIPSE and fdns) & int fund. Number yrs: b. Comps: a, c, d, e, g, k. Curr elem: a, b, c.

Missouri

Frank M. Patterson, English, **Central Missouri State University,** Warrensburg, MO 64093, (816) 429-4425. Pub, MA, 9,500 stud, int fund. Number yrs: a. Comps: g, k. Curr elem: d.

Margaret Muse and Donna Grout, **Lincoln University,** MLK 319, Jefferson City, MO 65101, (314) 681-5244. Pub, 4 yr, 2,400 stud, ext (Title III) & int fund. Number yrs: c. Comps: b, c, g, j, k.

Ann Canale, English, **Lindenwood College,** St. Charles, MO 63301, (314) 949-2000 x334. Priv, MA, 2,000 stud, int fund. Number yrs: a. Comps: b, g, k.

Ellen Forrest, Director, Plan & Dev, **Metropolitan Community Colleges,** 3200 Broadway, Kansas City, MO 64114, (816) 756-0220. Pub, cc, 13,500 stud, ext (Metropolitan Life Insurance Fdn) & int fund. Number yrs: b. Comps: b, c, e, g, h, j, k, l.

Joseph Lambert, English, **Missouri Southern State College,** Joplin, MO 64801-1595, (417) 625-9377. Int fund. Number yrs: a. Comp: f. Curr elem: a, b, c.

Elizabeth Latosi-Sawin, **Missouri Western State College,** 4525 Downs Dr, St. Joseph, MO 64507, (816) 271-4274. Pub, 4 yr, 4,000 stud, int fund. Number yrs: c. Comps: a, b, e, h, i, j, l.

Shirley Morahan, **Northeast Missouri State University,** Kirksville, MO 63501, (816) 785-4494. Pub, MA, 6,000 stud, int fund. Number yrs: d. Comps: a, d, k. Curr elem: b.

Sarah Morgan, **Park College,** Parkville, MO 64152, (816) 741-2000 x334. Priv, 4yr, ext (Title III) & int fund. Number yrs: d. Comps: e, h, k. Curr elem: a, d.

Phil Garman, Director, Ctr for Writing & Thinking, **School of the Ozarks,** Point Lookout, MO 65726, (417) 334-6411. Priv, 4 yr, 1,100 stud, ext (Hazen Fdn, Pew Memorial Trust) & int fund. Number yrs: c. Comps: a, b, e, g, j, k, l. Curr elem: b.

Doug Hunt, **University of Missouri,** 319 Gen'l Classrm Bldg, **Columbia,** MO 65211, (314) 882-4881. Pub, PhD, 22,000 stud, ext (NEH) & int fund. Number yrs: c. Comps: a, c, d, e, f, h, i, j, k. Curr elem: c.

Robert F. Wilson, Jr, English, **University of Missouri** 106 CH, **Kansas City,** MO 64110-2499, (816) 276-2766. Pub, PhD, int fund. Number yrs: a. Comps: b, c, d, e, g, i, k. Curr elem: b, c.

John A. Cannteson, **William Jewell College,** Liberty, MO 64068, (816) 781-3806. Pub, 4 yr, 1,400 stud. Number yrs: e. Comps: e, i, j, k. Curr elem: a, c, e.

Montana

John Ramage and Mark Waldo, English, **Montana State University,** Bozeman, MT 59717, (406) 994-3768. Pub, PhD, 9,600 stud, ext (FIPSE) & int fund. Number yrs: d. Comps: a, b, c, d, e, k, l. Curr elem: a.

Kenneth Egan, Jr, English, **Rocky Mountain College**, 1511 Poly Dr, Billings, MT 59102, (406) 657-1095. Priv, 4 yr, 560 stud, int fund. Number yrs: c. Comps: b, d, i, j, k. Curr elem: a.

Henry R. Harrington, English, **University of Montana**, Missoula, MT 59802, (406) 243-5231. Pub, PhD, 9,000 stud, ext (NEH) & int fund. Number yrs: c. Comps: a, d, f, k. Curr elem: a, c, d.

Nebraska

G. N. Bergquist, English & Speech, **Creighton University**, Omaha, NE 68178, (402) 280-2822. Priv, PhD, 5,900 stud, ext (gift) & int fund. Number yrs: b. Comps: b, c, j, k. Curr elem: a, b.

David Anderson, Writ Ctr, **Kearney State College**, Thomas 104, Kearney, NE 68849, (308) 234-8641. Pub, MA, 9,000 stud, ext (Title III) and int fund. Number yrs: a. Comps: a, c, e, f, g, h, j, k. Curr elem: a, b, c, d.

Leon Satterfield, **Nebraska Wesleyan**, Lincoln, NE 68504, (402) 465-2350. Priv, 4 yr, 1,200 stud, ext fund (CAPHE). Number yrs: a. Comps: a, b, c, j.

New Hampshire

Jane Cooke, Ellen Stowers, and David Elderkin, **Hesser College**, 25 Lowell St, Manchester, NH 03101, (603) 668-6660. Priv, int fund. Number yrs: a. Comps: b, c, e, g, j, k. Curr elem: a, b, c.

Mary-Lou Hinman, **Plymouth State College**, Plymouth, NH 03264, (603) 536-3201 x2598. Pub, 4 yr, 3,500 stud, int fund. Number yrs: c. Comps: a, c, f, g, h, i, j, k. Curr elem: a, c.

Thomas Newkirk, English, **University of New Hampshire**, Hamilton Smith Hall, Durham, NH 03824, (603) 862-3965. Pub, PhD, 10,500 stud, int fund. Number yrs: a. Comps: b.

New Jersey

Thomas F. Boghosian, **Atlantic Community College**, Mays Landing, NJ 08330, (609) 343-4967. Pub, cc, 2,500 stud, ext (NJ Dept. of Higher Ed) & int fund. Number yrs: b. Comps: a, c, i, j, l.

Michael A. Orlando, **Bergen Community College**, 400 Paramus Rd, Paramus, NJ 07652-1595, (201) 664-0172. Pub, cc, 10,000 stud, int fund. Number yrs: c. Comps: b, c, e, i, k.

Freda Hepner, Applied Humanities, **Brookdale Community College**, Newman Springs Road, Lincroft, NJ 07738, (609) 448-4344. Pub, cc, 12,000 stud, ext (FICE-DHE) & int fund. Number yrs: c. Comps: a, b, c, e, g, h, i, j, k, l.

John Seabrook, **Essex County College**, Newark, NJ 07102, (201) 877-1867. Pub, cc, 5,007 stud, ext (FIPSE) & int fund. Number yrs: d.

Richard Katz, **Kean College of New Jersey**, Union, NJ 07083, (201) 527-2399. Pub, 4 yr, 13,000 stud, ext (state) & int funds. Number yrs: a. Comps: a, c, e, f, g, h, i, j, k. Curr elem: a, c.

Vera Goodkin, Humanities & Social Sciences, **Mercer County Community College**, PO Box B, Trenton, NJ 08690. Pub. cc, 8,423 stud, int fund. Number yrs: e. Comps: a, b, c, e, f, g, i, j, k, l.

Caryl K. Sills, Writing Director, **Monmouth College**, West Branch, NJ 07764, (201) 571-3620. Priv, 4 yr, 4,500 stud, ext (DHE grant) & int fund. Number yrs: a. Comps: b, c, e, g, k.

Jerome Paris, Humanities, **New Jersey Institute of Technology**, 323 King Blvd, Newark, NJ 07102, (201) 596-3373, 3268. Pub, PhD, 4,000 stud, ext fund (NJ Dept of Higher Ed). Number yrs: c. Comps: a, b, c, h, j.

Katherine T. Hoff, **Rider College**, 2083 Lawrenceville Rd, Lawrenceville, NJ 08648-3099, (609) 895-5571, 896-5145. Priv, 4 yr, 4,000 stud, ext (NJ Dept. of Higher Ed) & int fund. Number yrs: d. Comps: a, b, c, h, j, k.

Karen Jahn, English, **St. Peter's College**, Jersey City, NJ 07306, (201) 333-4400. Priv, 4 yr, 1,800 stud, ext fund (NJ Dept. of Higher Ed). Number yrs: c. Comps: a, c, e, h, i, j, k, l.

Jack Connor, Director of Writing, **Stockton State College**, Pomona, NJ 08240, (609) 652-4712. Pub, 4 yr, 5,000 stud, int fund. Number yrs: d. Comps: b, k. Curr elem: b, c.

Donna Perry, WAC, & Sally Hand, English, **William Paterson College**, Matelson Hall, Wayne, NJ 07470, (201) 595-3068 x2214, 2254. Pub, 4 yr, 10,000 stud, ext (NJ Dept of Higher Ed) & int fund. Number yrs: c. Comps: a, b, c, g, h, i, j, k. Curr elem: a, b, c.

New Mexico

Christopher C. Burnham, English, **New Mexico State University**, Box 3E, Las Cruces, NM 88003, (505) 646-3931. Pub, PhD, 14,000 stud, ext (NEH) & int fund. Number yrs: d. Comps: a, c, h, i, l.

New York

Leonare Hoffman, English, **Borough of Manhattan Community College**, 199 Chambers St, New York, NY 10007, (212) 618-1520. Pub, cc, 12,000 stud, int fund. Number yrs: c. Comps: a, c, g, h, i, j.

Marsha Z. Cummins, English, **Bronx Community College CUNY**, University Ave & W 181st Street, Bronx, NY 10453, (212) 220-6947. Pub, cc, 6,131 stud, ext (NY Voc Ed Act, NEH) & int fund. Number yrs: a. Comps: a, b, c, e, j, k, l.

Patricia Bernadt Durfee, English, **Broome Community College**, Binghamton, NY 13904, (607) 771-5081. Pub, cc, 3,500 stud, int fund. Number yrs: d. Comps: b, c, e, f, j, k. Curr elem: a.

Janet S. Forsman, English, **Clinton Community College**, Plattsburgh, NY 12901, (518) 6650 x383. Pub, cc, 1,750 stud, int fund. Number yrs: b. Comps: b, e, g, h, i, k. Curr elem: b.

The Interdisciplinary Writing Program, **Colgate University**, Hamilton, NY 13346, (315) 824-1000 x375. Priv, 4 yr, 2,600 stud, int fund. Number yrs: c. Comps: b, g, i, j, k, l. Curr elem: d.

April Selley, **College of Saint Rose**, Box 125, Albany, NY 12203, (518) 454-5221. Priv, MA, 2,100 stud, int fund. Number yrs: c. Comps: b, c, g, h, j, k.

Joan E. Hartman, English, **College of Staten Island CUNY**, Staten Island, NY 10301. Pub, MA, 1,100 stud, ext (Title III) & int fund. Number yrs: b. Comps: k.

Martha Afzal, **Dutchess Community College**, Poughkeepsie, NY 12601, (914) 471-4500 x3403. Pub, cc, 7,000 stud, int fund. Number yrs: a. Comps: g, k. Curr elem: c.

John H. O'Neill, Director, Reading-Writing Ctr, English, **Hamilton College**, Clinton, NY 13323, (315) 859-4463, 4361. Priv, 1,600 stud, ext fund (Christian Johnson Endeavor Fdn). Number yrs: a. Comps: a, c, e, f, j, k. Curr elem: a, c.

Robert R. Benson, Director of Writing, **Hartwick College**, Oneonta, NY 13820, (607) 432-4200. Priv, 4 yr, 1,400 stud, ext (NEH) & int fund. Number yrs. e. Comps: b, c, k. Curr elem: a, c.

Tamar March, **Hobart & William Smith Colleges**, Geneva, NY 14456, (315) 789-1895. Priv, 4 yr, 1,900 stud, int fund. Number yrs: b. Comps: a, c, g, i. Curr elem: a, b, d.

Linda Hirsch, **Hostos Community College, CUNY**, 500 Grand Concourse Rd, Bronx, NY 10451, (212) 960-1328. Pub, cc, 4,500 stud, ext (FIPSE) & int fund. Number yrs: d. Comps: a, b, c, j.

Helen Bauer, **Iona College**, New Rochelle, NY 10801, (914) 633-2401. Priv, 4 yr, 4,000 stud, int fund. Number yrs: c. Comps: a, c, d, e, j, k.

Catherine S. Penner, Coordinator, Writing Prog., **Ithaca College**, Muller 102D, Ithaca, NY 14850, (607) 274-3470. Priv, 4 yr, 5,700 stud, int fund. Number yrs: a. Comps: a, b, e, f, g, i, j, k. Curr elem: a, b, c, d.

David Seguin, **Jamestown Community College**, Jamestown, NY 14701, (716) 665-5220 x319. Pub, cc, 3,500 stud, ext fund (JCC Fdn). Number yrs: a. Comps: b, f.

JoAnn Anderson and Nora Eisenberg, **LaGuardia Community College**, Long Island City, NY 11101, (718) 482-5410. Pub, cc, ext (Title III, St Dept of Higher Ed, fdns, City University) & int fund. Number yrs: e. Comps: a.

David Lloyd, English, **Le Moyne College**, Syracuse, NY 13214, (315) 455-4386. Priv, 4 yr, 1,900 stud, int fund. Number yrs: d. Comps: k. Curr elem: a.

Joseph Dorinson, History, **Long Island University, Zeckendorf Campus**, Brooklyn, NY 11201, (718) 403-1057. Priv, 4 yr, 2,600 stud, int fund. Number yrs: a. Comps: f, g, h, i, k.

Lorna D. Edmundson, Acad Dean, **Marymount College**, Tarrytown, NY 10591, (914) 631-3200. Priv, 4 yr, 1,200 stud, int fund. Number yrs: c. Comps: a, c, d, e, f, g, i, j, k. Curr elem: a, b, c, d.

Elizabeth D. Harrell, **Medgar Evers College**, 1150 Carroll St, Brooklyn, NY 11225, (718) 735-1801, 1802. Pub, cc, 2,500 stud, ext fund (Title III). Number yrs: c. Comps: b.

Martha Nockimson, **Mercy College**, Dobbs Ferry, NY 10522. Priv, 4 yr, 7,000 stud, int fund. Number yrs: b. Comps: a, b, c, e, g, i, j.

Thomas Giometti, **Mohawk Valley Community College**, Utica, NY 13501, (315) 792-5508. Pub, cc, 5,000 stud, int fund. Number yrs: a. Comps: a, c, e, f, g, h, i, j. Curr elem: a, c.

Stasia J. Callan, English, **Monroe Community College**, Rochester, NY 14623, (716) 424-5200 x3370, 3382. Pub, cc, 11,000 stud, int fund. Number yrs: c. Comps: a, b, c, e, j. Curr elem: c.

Deborah A. Dooley, English, **Nazareth College of Rochester**, 4245 East Ave, Rochester, NY 14610, (716) 586-2525 x537 or 262. Priv, 4 yr, 1,475 stud, int fund. Number yrs: a. Comps: a, c, e, f, i, k. Curr elem: c.

Harriet E. Spitzer, Humanities, **New York Institute of Technology**, Wheatley Rd, Old Westbury, NY 11568, (516) 686-7712. Priv, 4 yr, 13,000 stud, ext (Title III) & int fund. Number yrs: a. Comps: b, c, e, g.

Rita Pollard, English, **Niagara University**, Niagara, NY 14109, (716) 285-1212 x580. Priv, MA, 2,700 stud, int fund. Number yrs: a. Comps: a, b, c, e, g, i, j, k. Curr elem: a.

Christine Godwin, Writing Consultancy Proj, **Orange County Community College**, Middletown, NY 10940, (914) 343-1121 x2065. Pub, cc, 4,456 stud, ext (VEA, St University of NY) & int fund. Number yrs: e. Comps: a, b, c, e, k. Curr elem: d.

Wolhee Choe, Humanities, **Polytechnic University,** 333 Jay St., Brooklyn, NY 11201, (718) 260-3402. Priv, PhD, 5,000 stud, ext (NEH) and int fund. Number yrs: d. Comps: i, k. Curr elem: a.

Linda C. Stanley, English, **Queensborough Community College,** Bayside, NY 11364. Pub, cc, 11,000 stud, ext fund (St Dept of Higher Ed). Number yrs: d. Comps: b, c, e, f, g, h, i, k, l.

Cheryl Geisler, Lang, Lit, & Comm, **Rensselaer Polytechnic Inst,** Troy, NY 12180, (518) 276-2724. Priv, PhD, 4,500 stud, ext & int fund. Number yrs: b. Comps: b, c, d, f, k. Curr elem: c.

Joseph Nassar, Lib Arts, **Rochester Institute of Technology,** Rochester, NY 14623, (716) 475-2442. Priv, MA, 12,000 stud, int fund. Number yrs: c. Comps: b, e, f, j, k. Curr elem: c.

Nancy Leech, Writing Ctr Director, **Rockland Community College,** 145 College Rd, Suffern, NY 10901, (914) 356-4650 x426. Pub, cc, int fund. Number yrs: b. Comps: b, c, e, f, k.

Gladys M. Craig, English, **Russell Sage College,** Troy, NY 12180, (518) 270-2237. Priv, 4 yr, 1,000 stud, int fund. Number yrs: a. Comps: b, c, e.

Thomas Hemmeter, English, **St. Lawrence University,** Canton, NY 13617, (315) 379-5898. Priv, 4 yr, 2,200 stud, int fund. Number yrs: a. Comps: j, k. Curr elem: a.

Philip Boshoff, English, **Skidmore College,** Saratoga Springs, NY 12866, (518) 584-5000 x2551. Priv, 4 yr, 2,100 stud, ext (NEH) and int fund. Number yrs: e. Comps: a, b, c, j, k, l. Curr elem: a, c.

Steve North, English, **State University of New York, Albany,** NY 12222, (518) 442-4069. Pub, PhD, 16,000 stud, int fund. Number yrs: d. Comps: b, c, d, e, h, i, j, k. Curr elem: c.

Patricia Speyser, English, **State University of New York, Binghamton,** NY 13901, (607) 777-2085. Int fund. Number yrs: e. Comps: b, d, e, k. Curr elem: c, d.

Paul Curran, **State University of New York, Brockport,** NY 14420, (716) 395-5234. Pub, 4 yr, 8,000 stud, ext (Title III) & int fund. Number yrs: e. Comps: a, b, e, j, k. Curr elem: a.

Ann R. Shapiro, English, Whitman Hall, **State University of New York, Farmingdale,** NY 11735, (516) 420-2190. Number yrs: a. Comps: a, b, j.

Patrick L. Courts, English, **State University of New York, Fredonia,** NY 14063, (716) 673-3450, 3125. Pub, 4 yr, 4,800 stud, int fund. Number yrs: d. Comps: a, c. Curr elem: b, c.

Joel J. Belson, **State University of New York Maritime College,** Fort Schuyler, Bronx, NY 10425, (212) 409-7248. Pub, 4 yr, 850 stud, int fund. Number yrs: e. Comps: c, i, l. Curr elem: b, c, d.

Jan Schmidt, English, **State University of New York, New Paltz,** NY 12561, (914) 257-2452, 2383. Pub, MA, 7,000 stud, int fund. Comps: b, c, i, j. Curr elem: b.

Thomas Morrissey, English, **State University of New York, Plattsburgh,** NY 12901, (518) 564-2134. Pub, 4 yr, 5,300 stud, int fund. Number yrs: c. Comps: b, c, f, i, l. Curr elem: c.

Allan Duane, English, **Ulster County Community College,** Stone Ridge, NY 12484, (914) 687-7621 x402. Pub, cc, 2,500 stud, ext (Voc Ed Grant) & int fund. Number yrs: b. Comps: b, c, g, j. Curr elem: c.

Col. Frank Giondana, Math, **U.S. Military Academy, West Point,** NY 10996-1786. Pub, 4 yr, 4,400 stud. Number yrs: d. Comps: b, f, k. Curr elem: a, c.

Carolyn Kirkpatrick, English, and Jo Lewis, Sociology, **York College, CUNY,** Jamaica, NY 11451, (718) 262-2470, 2605. Pub, 4 yr, 4,500 stud, ext (Title III) & int fund. Number yrs: a. Comps: a, f, h, i, j. Curr elem: c.

North Carolina

Anthony Gritta, **Davidson County Community College**, PO Box 1287, Lexington, NC 27292, (704) 249-8186. Pub, cc, 2,000 stud, int fund. Number yrs: b. Comps: i, k.

George D. Gopen, **Duke University**, 307 Allen Bldg, Durham, NC 27706, (919) 684-8877. Priv, PhD, 7,000 stud, int fund. Number yrs: a. Comps: a, c, d, e, k. Curr elem: a, b, c, d.

Patrick Bizzaro, English, **East Carolina University**, Greenville, NC 27834, (919) 757-6576. Pub, MA, 4,000 stud, int fund. Number yrs: a. Comps: b, c, e, g, j, k. Curr elem: a.

Monika L. Sutherland, English, **Edgecombe Technical College**, Tarbor, NC 27886. Pub, cc, 1,000 stud, int fund. Number yrs: a. Comps: b, j, k. Curr elem: b.

Barbara Gordon, **Elon College**, Box 2550, Elon College, NC 27244, (919) 584-2123. Priv, 4 yr, 3,500 stud, int fund. Number yrs: c. Comps: a, b, c, e, j. Curr elem: a.

Jeff Jeske, English, **Guilford College**, Greensboro, NC 27410, (919) 292-5511 x216. Priv, 4 yr, 1,500 stud, int fund. Number yrs: a. Comps: b, e, j, k. Curr elem: a, b, c.

Phyllis A. Barber, English & Humanities, **Guilford Technical Institute**, PO Box 309, Jamestown, NC 27282, (919) 292-1101 x2492 or 2203. Pub, cc, 5,000 stud, ext fund (state). Number yrs: a. Comps: a, c, g, h, i, j, k, l. Curr elem: d.

James D. Williams, English, **University of North Carolina**, Greenlaw Hall CB 3520, **Chapel Hill**, NC 27514, (919) 962-5481. Pub, PhD, 18,000 stud, ext fund (Ford Fdn). Number yrs: a. Comps: a, b, c, d, e, g, k. Curr elem: a.

Sam Watson, English, **University of North Carolina, Charlotte**, NC 28223, (704) 547-4216. Pub, MA, 12,000 stud, int fund. Number yrs: d. Comps: a, c, e, f, g, h, i, j, k, l. Curr elem: b, c.

Liz Meador and Marian Westbrook, **Wayne Community College**, Caller Box 8002, Goldsboro, NC 27533-8002, (919) 735-5151 x251 or 313. Pub, cc, 1,200 stud, int fund. Number yrs: a. Comps: b, c, e, k.

Blair M. Hancock, **Wilkes Community College**, PO Box 120, Wilkesboro, NC 28697, (919) 667-7136. Pub, cc, 3,000 stud, int fund. Number yrs: b. Comps: b, c, g, j, k.

Robert Doak, **Wingate College**, Box 3008, Wingate, NC 28174, (704) 233-8080. Priv, 4 yr, 1,600 stud, int fund. Number yrs: a. Comps: a. Curr elem: c.

North Dakota

Muhammad Ndaula, **Standing Rock College**, Fort Yates, ND 58538, (701) 854-3861. Pub, cc, 300 stud, ext fund. Number yrs: b. Comps: k. Curr elem: c, d.

Ohio

Thomas D. Klein, English, **Bowling Green State University**, Bowling Green, OH 43403, (419) 372-2576. Pub, PhD, 6,000 stud, int fund. Number yrs: b. Comps: a, c, g, i, j, k.

JoAnne M. Podis, **Dyke College**, 112 Prospect Ave, Cleveland, OH 44114, (216) 523-3843. Priv, 4 yr, 1,300 stud, ext (Cleveland Fdn) & int fund. Number yrs: b. Comps: b, j.

Mary Harris, Assoc. Dean, Lib Arts, **Edison State Community College**, 1973 Edison Drive, Piqua, OH 45356, (513) 778-8600. Pub, cc, 2,400 stud, int fund. Number yrs: b. Comps: b, c, e, f, k.

Howard P. Erlichman, **Lakeland Community College**, Mentor, OH 44060, (216) 953-7187. Pub, cc, 8,451 stud, int fund. Number yrs: c. Comps: a, c, j. Curr elem: a.

Susan G. Luck, **Lorain County Community College**, 1005 N Abbe Rd, Elyria, OH 44035, (216) 734-4600 x 532. Pub, cc, ext (OH Board of Regents) & int fund. Number yrs: a. Comps: b, c, g, k.

Burley Smith, Lang & Lit, **Malone College**, Canton, OH 44709, (216) 489-0800 x461. Priv, 4 yr, 1,000 stud, ext fund (Glenmede Fdn). Number yrs: a. Comps: a, b, c, f, i, j, k, l.

William J. Schultz, English, **Muskingum College**, New Concord, OH 43762, (614) 826-8266. Priv, 4 yr, 1,000 stud, ext (East Central College Consortium, Gund Fdn) & int fund. Number yrs: d. Comps: a, c, j. Curr elem: c.

Betty P. Pytlik, English, **Ohio University**, Athens, OH 45701, (614) 593-2836. Pub, PhD, 1,500 stud, int fund. Number yrs: d. Comps: a, b, c, e, f, g, i, l. Curr elem: c.

Dean of Acad Affairs, **Ohio Wesleyan University**, Delaware, OH 43015. Priv, 4 yr, 1,650 stud. Number yrs: b. Comps: a, e. Curr elem: c.

Joan A. Mullins, Director, Writing Ctr, **University of Toledo**, 2801 W Bancroft, Toledo, OH 43606, (419) 537-4913. Pub, PhD, 21,700 stud, int fund. Number yrs: a. Comps: b, c, e, g, j, k. Curr elem: a, d.

Janet Minc, **Wayne General and Technical College**, 10470 Smucker Rd, Orrville, OH 44313, (216) 683-2010. Pub, cc, 1,200 stud, ext fund (st acad challenge grant). Number yrs: b. Comps: b, e, g, h, i, j, k.

Mimi Still Dixon, English, **Wittenberg University**, Springfield, OH 45501, (513) 327-7066. Priv, 4 yr, 2,250 stud, int fund. Number yrs: e. Comps: b, c, d, e, f, h, j, k. Curr elem: c.

Richard H. Bullock, Director of Writing Prog, **Wright State University**, Dayton, OH 45435, (513) 873-2220. Pub, PhD, 10,000 stud, ext (NEH) & int fund.Number yrs: a. Comps: a, b, c, e, j, k. Curr elem: a.

Oklahoma

Lyle D. Olson, **Bartlesville Wesleyan College**, 2201 Silver Lake Rd, Bartlesville, OK 74006, (918) 333-6151 x282. Priv, 4 yr, 325 stud. Number yrs: b. Comps: b, c.

Kevin Davis, Writ Ctr Director, **East Central University**, Ada, OK 74820, (405) 332-8000 x449. Pub, MA, 4,000 stud, int fund. Number yrs: c. Comps: b, c, e, f, h, j, k. Curr elem: a.

Terry Phelps, Writing Center, **Oklahoma City University**, 2501 N. Blackwelder, Oklahoma City, OK 73106, (405) 521-5040. Priv, MA, 3,400 stud, ext fund (donors). Number yrs: a. Comps: b, j, k. Curr elem: c.

Clyta F. Harris, English, **Oral Roberts University**, 7777 S Lewis Ave, Tulsa, OK 74171, (918) 495-6760. Priv, MA, 4,300 stud, int fund. Number yrs: a. Comps: b, c, i, k. Curr elem: b.

Michael C. Flanigan, English, **University of Oklahoma**, Norman, OK 73019, (405) 325-4661. Pub, PhD, 15,000 stud, int fund. Number yrs: b. Comps: a, b, i. Curr elem: a, b.

Oregon

Marilyn A. Dyrud, **Oregon Institute of Technology**, Klamath Falls, OR 97601, (503) 882-6991. Pub, 4 yr, 3,000 stud. Number yrs: b. Comps: b, c, f, h, i, j. Curr elem: b, c.

Greg Jacob, Director of Writing Ctr, **Pacific University**, Forest Grove, OR 97116, (503) 357-6151 x2250. Priv, 4 yr, 1,200 stud, int fund. Number yrs: b. Comps: c, e, k.

Ulrich H. Hardt, Sec'y to the Faculty, **Portland State University**, PO Box 751, Portland, OR 97207. Pub, PhD, 17,000 stud, int fund. Number yrs: a. Comps: b, e, j, k. Curr elem: c.

John Gage, English, **University of Oregon,** Eugene, OR 97403-1286. Pub, PhD, 13,000 stud, ext (NEH) and int fund. Number yrs: d. Comps: b, k. Curr elem: a, b.

Richard L. Caulkins, **Western Baptist College**, 5000 Deer Park Dr SE, Salem, OR 97302, (503) 581-8600. Priv, 4 yr, 288 stud, int fund. Number yrs: b. Comps: b, c, e, k. Curr elem: a, b.

Pennsylvania

Susan Belasco Smith, Director of Comp, **Allegheny College**, PO Box 110, Meadville, PA 16335, (814) 724-2351. Priv, 4 yr, 1,900 stud, int fund. Number yrs: d. Comps: b, c, e, k, l.

Jo Ann Bomze, **Beaver College**, Glenside, PA 19038, (215) 572-2105. Priv, 4 yr, 800 stud, ext (NEH) & int fund. Number yrs: e. Comps: a, b, c, d, j, k, l. Curr elem: a.

M. Lois Huffines, Mod Lang, **Bucknell University**, Roberts Hall, Lewisburg, PA 17837, (717) 524-3141. Priv, 4 yr, 3,465 stud, ext (NEH) & int fund. Number yrs: e. Comps: a, b, c, e, f, h, i, j, k, l.

Marilyn J. Puchalski, **Bucks County Community College**, Swamp Road, Newton, PA 18940, (215) 968-8293. Pub, cc, 9,000 stud, int fund. Number yrs: d. Comps: b, d, e, g, h, j, k. Curr elem: a.

Jerome Zurek, **Cabrini College**, Radnor, PA 19087, (215) 971-8360. Priv, 4 yr, 800 stud. Number yrs: d. Comps: a, b, j, k. Curr elem: a, c.

Jane Gerety, English, **Carlow College**, Pittsburgh, PA 15213, (412) 578-6029. Priv, 4 yr, 800 stud, int fund. Number yrs: c. Comps: b, j, k.

Richard E. Young, English, **Carnegie-Mellon University**, Pittsburgh, PA 15213, (412) 268-6451, 2850. Priv, PhD, 6,000 stud, ext (Pew Fdn) & int fund. Number yrs: b. Comps: b, c, f, j, l. Curr elem: a.

Karyn Hollis, **Dickinson College**, Carlisle, PA 17013, (717) 245-1745. Priv, 4 yr, 1,900 stud, int fund. Number yrs: b. Comps: a, b, c, f, g, j, k. Curr elem: a, b, c.

John F. Ennis, **King's College**, Wilkes-Barre, PA 18711, (717) 826-5900. Priv, 4 yr, 1,750 stud, ext (Title III) & int fund. Number yrs: e. Comps: a, c, g, k, l.

Patricia Donahue, English, **Lafayette College,** Easton, PA 18042, (215) 252-8315. Priv, 4 yr, 2,000 stud, int fund. Number yrs: b. Comps: b, c, d, e, j, l.

Margot Soven, English, **La Salle University**, Philadelphia, PA 19141, (215) 951-1148, 1145. Priv, 4 yr, 3,500 stud, ext fund (NEH). Number yrs: e. Comps: a, b, c, d, h, i, j, k, l. Curr elem: a, c.

Joanne D. Gerken, **Lehigh County Community College,** 2370 Main St, Schnecksville, PA 18078, (215) 799-1186. Pub, cc, 2,000 stud, ext fund (Title III). Number yrs: a. Comps: b, c, e, j, k.

Rosemary J. Mundhenk, English, **Lehigh University**, Maginnes #9, Bethlehem, PA 18015, (215) 758-3310. Priv, PhD, 1,100 stud, ext (NEH) & int fund. Number yrs: d. Comps: a, c, e, g, j, k. Curr elem: b, c.

Marie A. Nigra, **Lincoln University,** Lincoln, PA 19352 (215) 932-8300 x518. Pub, MA, 1,100 stud, ext & int fund. Number yrs: a. Comps: b, c, e, i, j, k. Curr elem: b, c.

Walter Sanders, English, **Mansfield University,** Belknap Hall, Mansfield, PA 16933, (717) 662-4592. Pub, MA, 2,300 stud, int fund. Number yrs: a. Comps: b, c, e, f, i, j, k. Curr elem: a, b, c.

Donald Wolff, Humanities, **Penn State University—Harrisburg,** Middletown, PA 17057, (717) 948-6191. Pub, MA, 2,900 stud, int fund. Number yrs: a. Comps: e, h, k. Curr elem: b.

Mary M. Dupvis, University Writing Cmte, **Penn State University,** 145 Chambers Bldg, **University Park,** PA 16802, (814) 865-6321. Pub, PhD, 45,000 stud, int fund. Number yrs: a. Comps: b, c, f. Curr elem: c.

Jo Ann M. Sipple, Director, Writing Across the Business Disciplines, **Robert Morris College,** 5th Ave at 6th, Pittsburgh, PA 15219, (412) 262-8285, 227-6859. Priv, 4 yr, 6,000 stud, ext (Buhl Fdn) & int fund. Number yrs: d. Comps: a, b, c, e, f, h, i, j, l. Curr elem: c.

Robert Dunn, **St. Joseph's University,** Philadelphia, PA 19131. Priv, 4 yr, 2,300 stud, int fund. Number yrs: e. Comps: b, k.

Robert McIlvaine, English, **Slippery Rock University,** Slippery Rock, PA 16057, (412) 794-7232. Pub, MA, 6,200 stud, ext (state) & int fund. Number yrs: c. Comps: a, b, g, h, j, k. Curr elem: b, c.

Thomas H. Blackburn, English, **Swarthmore College,** 609 Elm Ave, Swarthmore, PA 19081. Priv, 4 yr, 1,300 stud, int fund. Number yrs: c. Comps: c, d. Curr elem: c.

Stephen Zelnick, English, **Temple University,** Philadelphia, PA 19122, (215) 787-5059. Pub, PhD, 31,000 stud, int fund. Number yrs: a. Comps: b, f. Curr elem: a, b, c.

Peshe Kuriloff, **University of Pennsylvania,** 413A Bennett Hall, Philadelphia, PA 19104-6273, (215) 898-4566. Priv, PhD, 8,000 stud, ext (fdns, gifts) & int fund. Number yrs: c. Comps: d, i, j, k. Curr elem: c.

David Bartholmae, English, **University of Pittsburgh**, Pittsburgh, PA 15260, (412) 624-6530. Pub, PhD, 2,500 stud, int fund. Number yrs: e. Comps: c, f, h, k. Curr elem: c.

John T. Young, **Villa Maria College,** 2551 W Lake Rd, Erie, PA 16505, (814) 838-1966 x254. Priv, 4 yr, 600 stud, int fund. Number yrs: c. Comps: b, c, e, j, k. Curr elem: a.

Robert Weiss, **West Chester University,** 210 Philips Bldg, West Chester, PA 19383, (215) 436-2297. Pub, MA, 11,000 stud, ext (NEH) & int fund. Number yrs: e. Comps: a, b, f, h, j, k. Curr elem: c.

Rhode Island

Tori Haring-Smith, **Brown University,** Box 1852, Providence, RI 02912, (401) 863-1404. Priv, PhD, 7,000 stud, ext (private fdns) & int fund. Number yrs: d. Comps: a, c, d, f, k. Curr elem: c.

Mary McGann, Writing Center, **Rhode Island College,** Providence, RI 02908, (401) 456-8678. Pub, 4 yr, 6,000 stud, ext (state governor's office) and int fund. Number yrs: d. Comps: a, c, f, i, j, k. Curr elem: a.

South Dakota

Stewart Bellman, **Black Hills State College,** Box 9052, Spearfish, SD 57783, (605) 642-6860. Pub, 4 yr, 2,100 stud, int fund. Number yrs: d. Comps: b, c, e, f, k.

Ruth Foreman and Mary Haug, **South Dakota State University,** NHE 253, Brookings, SD 57007, (605) 688-5191. Pub, 4 yr, 6,000 stud, ext (Dakota Writ Proj) & int fund. Number yrs: a. Comps: a, b.

Nancy T. Zuercher, English, **University of South Dakota**, 414 E Clark St, Vermillion, SD 57069, (605) 677-5229. Pub, PhD, 5,622 stud, int fund. Number yrs: b. Comps: a, b, c, i, j. Curr elem: b, c.

Tennessee

Ellen M. Millsaps, **Carson-Newman College**, Box 1865, Jefferson City, TN 37760, (615) 475-9061 x286. Priv, 4 yr, 1,800 stud, ext fund (Pew Fdn). Number yrs: a. Comps: a, b, c, e, j, k.

Carol Luther, **Hiwassee College**, Box 639, Madisonville, TN 37354, (615) 442-2520. Priv, 550 stud. Number yrs: a. Comps: g.

Nancy M. Fisher, **Roane State Community College**, Harriman, TN 37748, (615) 354-3000 x4237. Pub, cc, 4,000 stud, ext (st board grant) & int fund. Number yrs: d. Comps: b, c, e, g, h, j, k. Curr elem: a.

Kirsten Benson, **University of Tennessee**, 301 McClung Tower, Knoxville, TN 37996, (615) 974-6973. Pub, PhD, 25,000 stud, ext (Ford Fdn) & int fund. Number yrs: b. Comps: b, c, e, f, j, k. Curr elem: c.

Scott Colley, English, **Vanderbilt University**, Nashville, TN 37235, (615) 322-2542. Priv, PhD, 3,200 stud (Arts & Sciences), int fund. Number yrs: d. Comps: a, c, f, h, j, k.

Texas

Delryn R. Fleming, Comm Div, **Brookhaven College**, Farmers Branch, TX 75244, (214) 620-4772, 4770. Pub, cc, 8,500 stud, int fund. Number yrs: b. Comps: a, c, e, f, j, k.

Michael Burke, Comm & Dev Studies, **Eastfield College of Dallas County**, Mesquite, TX 75150-2099, (214) 324-7124. Int fund. Number yrs: b. Comps: d, i.

Agnes J. Robinson, **El Paso County Community College**, PO Box 20500, El Paso, TX 79998, (915) 534-4079. Pub, cc, 15,000 stud, int fund. Number yrs: c. Comps: a, g.

Cheryl Peters, WAC Director, Arts & Humanities, **Houston Community College System**, 320 Jackson Hill, Houston, TX 77007, (713) 868-0757. Pub, cc, 45,289 stud, int fund. Number yrs: c. Comps: d, e, f, h, i, j, k, l. Curr elem: a.

Joan Samuelson, **North Harris County College—East Campus**, Kingwood, TX 77339, (713) 359-1625. Pub, cc, 12,000 stud, int fund. Number yrs: b. Comps: a, b, e, f, g, h, j, k.

Joyce Powell, **Northlake College**, 5001 N MacArthur Rd, Irving, TX 75038-3899. Pub, cc, 5,800 stud, int fund. Number yrs: b. Comps: b, c, f, k. Curr elem: a.

Judith R. Lambert, Comm, **Richland College**, 12800 Abrams Rd, Dallas, TX 75243, (214) 238-6220. Ext (Arco Fdn) & int fund. Number yrs: d. Comps: a, b, g, h, i, j, l.

Marlin O. Cherry, Provost, **San Jacinto College District**, 4624 Fairmont Parkway, Suite 210, Pasadena, TX 77504, (713) 998-6110. Pub, cc, 17,000 stud, ext (TX Educ Agy) & int fund. Comps: b, c, d, g, j, k.

Schreiner College, Kerrville, TX 78028, (512) 896-5411 x256. Priv, 4 yr, 600 stud, int fund. Number yrs: a. Comps: a, b, e, j, k. Curr elem: a, b.

Randall Popken, English, **Tarleton State University**, Stephenville, TX 76402, (817) 968-9038. Pub, MA, 5,200 stud, int fund. Number yrs: c. Comps: k. Curr elem: a, b.

Tahita Fulkerson, English, **Tarrant County Junior College**, 4801 Marine Creek, Ft. Worth, TX 76179, (817) 232-2900. Pub, cc, 4,000 stud. Number yrs: b. Comps: b, e, k.

Levi Hall, Dean, **Texarkana College**, 2500 N Robinson Rd, Texarkana, TX 75501, (214) 838-4541. Pub, cc, 4,500 stud, int fund. Number yrs: a. Comps: b, c, j. Curr elem: d.

Neil Daniel, English, **Texas Christian University**, Box 32872, Ft. Worth, TX 76129, (817) 921-7240. Pub, PhD, 7,500 stud, int fund. Number yrs: a. Comps: a, b, c, f, h, i, j. Curr elem: c.

Frank Lewis, English, **Texas State Technical Institute**, Harlingen, TX 78550, (512) 425-0771. Pub, 2,300 stud, int fund. Number yrs: e. Comps: c. Curr elem: b.

Jon Harned, Arts & Humanities, **University of Houston—Downtown**, Houston, TX 77002, (713) 221-8112. Pub, 4 yr, 7,000 stud. Number yrs: a. Comps: a, c, e, g, i, k. Curr elem: a.

Feroza Jussawalla, English, **University of Texas**, Box 37, **El Paso**, TX 79968, (915) 747-5739. Pub, MA, 13,000 stud, ext (Ford Fdn) & int fund. Number yrs: c. Comps: l. Curr elem: a, c, d.

Utah

Sally T. Taylor, Director of Comp, **Brigham Young University**, 3112 JKHB, Provo, UT 84602, (801) 378-3565. Priv, PhD, 26,000 stud, int fund. Number yrs: e. Comps: a, b, f, j, k. Curr elem: a, b, c.

Janice W. Frost, University Writing Prog, **University of Utah**, 345 Orson Spencer Hall, Salt Lake City, UT 84112, (801) 581-5623, 7090. Pub, PhD, 23,000 stud, ext (NEH) & int fund. Number yrs: b. Comps: c, f, g, h, i, j. Curr elem: b, c.

Joyce Kinkead, Director of Writing, **Utah State University**, Logan, UT 84332-3200, (801) 750-2725. Pub, PhD, 12,000 stud, int fund. Number yrs: b. Comps: e, f, h, k, l. Curr elem: b, c.

Mark S. LeTourneau, **Weber State College**, 314 Social Science Bldg, Ogden, UT 84403, (801) 626-6081. Pub, 4 yr, 12,000 stud, int fund. Number yrs: a. Comps: a, b, d, g, h, i, k. Curr elem: b, c.

Vermont

Daniel J. Bean, Biology, **St. Michael's College**, Winooski, VT 05404, (802) 655-2000 x2622. Priv, 4 yr, 1,600 stud, int fund. Number yrs: a. Comps: a, b, d, j, k. Curr elem: b, c.

Toby Fulwiler, Director of Writing, **University of Vermont**, Burlington, VT 05405, (802) 656-3056. Pub, PhD, 11,000 stud, int fund. Number yrs: c. Comps: a, b, c, h, i, k, l.

Virginia

Douglas A. Petcher, English, **Blue Ridge Community College**, Weyers Cave, VA 24486, (703) 234-9261. Pub, cc, 2,000 stud, ext (VA St Council for Higher Ed). Number yrs: b. Comps: a, b, c, g, i, j.

Cheryl Guilinao, Director of Writing, **College of William & Mary**, Williamsburg, VA 23185, (804) 253-4370. Pub, PhD, int fund. Number yrs: b. Comps: d, e, f, g, k. Curr elem: c.

Christopher Thaiss, English, **George Mason University**, Fairfax, VA 22030, (703) 323-2220. Pub, PhD, 18,000 stud, ext (VA Funds for Excellence) & int fund. Number yrs: e. Comps: a, b, c, e, h, i, k, l. Curr elem: b, d.

Ellery Sedgwick, **Longwood College**, Farmville, VA 23901, (804) 392-9356. Pub, 4 yr, 2,700 stud, ext (NEH) & int fund. Number yrs: a. Comps: a, b, j, k. Curr elem: c.

Carol S. Manning, Writing Intensive Prog, **Mary Washington College**, Fredericksburg, VA 22401, (703) 899-4610. Pub, 4 yr, 3,200 stud, ext fund (state). Number yrs: d. Comps: a, b, e, g, i, j, k. Curr elem: a.

Johnny E. Tolliver, English & Foreign Lang, **Norfolk State University**, Norfolk, VA 23504, (804) 850-3335. Pub, MA, 7,500 stud, ext fund (Title III). Number yrs: c. Comps: a, b, f, g, j, k, l. Curr elem: a, b.

Northern Virginia Community College, Manassas Campus, 6901 Sudley Rd, Manassas, VA 22110. Pub, cc, 1,400 stud, int fund. Number yrs: c. Comps: b, e, f, j, k.

Kathleen L. Bell, English, **Old Dominion University**, Norfolk, VA 23508, (804) 440-4037, 3991. Pub, MA, 15,000 stud, int fund. Number yrs: c. Comps: a, c, g, i.

Richard J. Murphy, WAC Co-Coord, **Radford University**, Radford, VA 24142, (703) 831-5152. Pub, MA, 8,000 stud, ext (state) & int fund. Comps: a, b, c, g, h, i, j. Curr elem: c.

Dolly Tarver, English, **Virginia Highlands Community College**, Abingdon, VA 24210, (703) 628-6094. Pub, cc, 2,007 stud. Number yrs: b. Comps: k.

Washington

Karen Houck, English, **Bellevue Community College**, Box 92700, Bellevue, WA 98009-2037, (206) 641-2037. Pub, cc, int fund. Number yrs: b. Comps: a, b, c, f, i, j, k, l. Curr elem: c, d.

Sally Riewald, **Evergreen State College**, Tacoma Campus, 4106 N 30th, Tacoma, WA 98407, (206) 752-4827. Int fund. Number yrs: c. Comps: e, i. Curr elem: b.

Larry T. Blades, Humanities, **Highline Community College**, PO Box 98000, Des Moines, WA 98198-9800, (206) 878-3710 x439. Pub, cc, 9,000 stud, ext fund (NEH). Number yrs: b. Comps: b, f, j, k, l. Curr elem: a, d.

Marcia Barton, Humanities, **North Shore Community College**, 9600 College Way N, Seattle, WA 98103, (206) 527-3716, 3709. Pub, cc, 2,500 stud, int fund. Number yrs: d. Comps: a, b, c, j, l.

Luke M. Reinsma, Humanities, **Seattle Pacific University**, Seattle, WA 98119, (206) 281-2093. Priv, MA, 2,500 stud, ext fund (Pew Fdn). Number yrs: b. Comps: a, e, j, k. Curr elem: c.

John C. Bean, English, **Seattle University**, Seattle, WA 98122, (206) 296-5421. Priv, MA, 4,000 stud, ext (NW Area Fdn, Consort for Advmnt of Priv Higher Ed, corporate gifts) & int fund. Number yrs: b. Comps: a, b, c, d, e, i, j, k, l. Curr elem: a.

Lynn Dunlap, Lang & Lit, **Skagit Valley College**, 2405 College Way, Mount Vernon, WA 98273, (206) 428-1170, 1261. Pub, cc, 5,200 stud, int fund. Number yrs: a. Comps: b, c, e.

Julie Neff & Hans Ostrom, English, **University of Puget Sound**, Tacoma, WA 98416, (206) 756-3235, 3434. Priv, 4 yr, 2,800 stud, ext (Hearst Fdn) & int fund. Number yrs: e. Comps: a, c, e, i, j, k. Curr elem: a, c.

Joan Graham, Interdisc Writ Prog, English GN-30, **University of Washington**, Seattle, WA 98195, (206) 543-0758. Pub, PhD, 33,000 stud, ext (FIPSE, NEH) & int fund. Number yrs: e. Comps: a, b, c, d, e, f, i. Curr elem: c, d.

Susan Gardner and Bev Beem, **Walla Walla College**, College Place, WA 99324, (509) 527-2423. Priv, 4 yr, 1,600 stud, int fund. Number yrs: e. Comps: a, b, c, j, k. Curr elem: a, b, c, d.

Susan H. McLeod, Director of Comp, **Washington State University**, Pullman, WA 99164-5020, (509) 335-3022, 2581. Pub, PhD, 16,000 stud, int fund. Number yrs: b. Comps: a, b, c, e, f, j, k. Curr elem: a, c.

R. W. Fonda, Biology, **Western Washington University**, Bellingham, WA 98225, (206) 676-2911. Pub, MA, 8,250 stud, int fund. Number yrs: c. Comps: b, c, d, f, h, j, k. Curr elem: a, c.

C. Jean Carmean, **Whatcom Community College**, 237 W Kellogg Road, Bellingham, WA 98226, (206) 676-2170 x286. Pub, cc, 1,000 stud, int fund. Number yrs: d. Comps: a, b, c, e, f, g, i, j, l. Curr elem: d.

West Virginia

Robert M. Como, Lang Div, **Glenville State College**, Glenville, WV 26351, (304) 462-7361 x211. Pub, 4 yr, 2,000 stud, int fund. Number yrs: b. Comps: b, c, j. Curr elem: c.

Anita Gandolfo, English, **West Virginia University**, Morgantown, WV 26506, (304) 293-4460. Pub, PhD, 17,000 stud, int fund. Number yrs: a. Comps: b, c, e, i, k. Curr elem: d.

Wisconsin

Georgine Loacker, **Alverno College**, 3401 S 39 St, Milwaukee, WI 53215, (414) 382-6087. Priv, 4 yr, 1,982 stud, int fund. Number yrs: e. Comps: b, c, d, f, i, k. Curr elem: a, d.

Franklin M. Doeringer, Freshman Studies, **Lawrence University**, Appleton, WI 54912, (414) 735-6679. Priv, 4 yr, 1,100 stud, int fund. Number yrs: e. Comps: a, b, d, g, i, j, k. Curr elem: a.

Francis A. Hubbard, English, **Marquette University**, Milwaukee, WI 53012, (414) 224-7179. Priv, PhD, 14,000 stud, ext (Mellon Fdn) & int fund. Number yrs: c. Comps: a, b, c, i, j, k.

Ellen Kasulis, Learning Ctr, **Northland College**, Ashland, WI 54806, (715) 682-4531 x354. Priv, 4 yr, 586 stud, ext fund (TRIO prog). Number yrs: c. Comps: d, k. Curr elem: d.

James Korthals, Acad Dean, **Northwestern College**, 1300 Western Ave, Watertown, WI 53094, (414) 261-4352. Priv, 4 yr, 200 stud, int fund. Number yrs: a. Comps: b, c, j.

William Schang, **Ripon College**, 300 Seward St, PO Box 248, Ripon, WI 54971, (414) 748-8125. Int fund. Number yrs: b. Comps: a, b, c, e, i, j, k. Curr elem: c.

Ora L. M. Showers, **St. Norbert College**, De Pere, WI 54115, (414) 337-3062. Priv, 4 yr, 1,809 stud, int fund. Number yrs: e. Comps: b, e, h, k. Curr elem: b, c, d.

Mary Weiser, English, **University of Wisconsin, Eau Claire**, WI 54701, (715) 836-4953. Pub, MA, 11,200 stud, int fund. Number yrs: a. Comps: a.

Donald Pattow, English, **University of Wisconsin, Stevens Point**, WI 54481, (715) 346-4758. Pub, MA, 9,800 stud, ext fund (state). Number yrs: e. Comps: a, c, g, i, k. Curr elem: c.

Puerto Rico

Estela Lopez, Assoc V.P. Acad Affairs, **InterAmerican University**, GPO Box 3255, Central Admn, San Juan, PR, (809) 766-1912. Priv, MA, 39,000 stud, int fund. Number yrs: a. Comps: a, b, g.

Canada

Linda Shohet, Coord, Literacy Across the Curriculum, **Dawson College**, 350 Selby, Montreal, Quebec H3Z 1W7, (514) 931-8731, 8148. Pub, cc, 7,000 stud, ext (Ministry of Education) & int fund. Number yrs: c. Comps: b, c, e, g, h, i, j, k, l.

Christine Starnes, English, **John Abbott College**, PO 2000, Ste Anne de Bellevue, Quebec H9X 3L9, (514) 454-6610. Pub, cc, 4,930 stud, ext (prov govt) & int fund. Number yrs: d. Comps: b, c, g, h, k, l.

Colin J. Norman, English, **Queen's University**, Kingston, Ontario K7L 3C9, (613) 545-2153. Pub, PhD, 14,000 stud, int fund. Number yrs: c. Comps: b, c, d, e, g, i, j, k. Curr elem: a, d.

Susan H. McLeod is director of composition at Washington State University, where she initiated the writing across the curriculum program. She is a member of the board of consultants of the National Network of Writing Across the Curriculum Programs.

Susan Shirley has a degree in American Studies from Washington State University.

Index

D

Daly, J., 70, 74
D'Arcy, P., 85, 87, 96, 98, 102
Dartmouth Conference, 6
Darwin, C., 97
Davis, B. G., 74
Dawson Community College, newsletter of, 18
Departments: committees of, and curricular change, 10; at community colleges, 28; at research universities, 32-34; and second-stage workshops, 16
De Paul University, collaborative teaching at, 17-18
Dillard, A., 93
Disney, W., 47
Dobler, J. M., 83-84, 86
Doheny-Farina, S., 86, 87
Donovan, R., 73
Dowling, H. F., 80, 88
Drenk, D., 7, 12
Durfey, P., 23
Dyson, A. H., 48, 52

E

Education, collaborative research in, 82, 84-85
Eiseley, L., 93
Elbow, P., 68
El Paso County Community College, faculty institutes at, 27
Emig, J., 46, 52, 68, 92, 102
Empowerment, from writing, 92-93
English department faculty, writing taught by, 33-34, 100-101
Epistemology, at research universities, 35-36
ERIC documents, 73
Escalante, J., 47
Estes, T., 99, 102
Evaluation: aspects of, 61-75; background on, 61-62; barriers to, 62-64; bibliography on, 73-74; of community of scholars, 65-66; conclusions on, 72; of faculty writing, 71-72; measurable dimensions for, 64-72; of pedagogy, 66-68; of student learning, 68-69; of student writing, 69-71. See also Assessment

F

Faculty: centrality of, 101-102; at community colleges, 27-28; community of scholars for, 65-66, 99-100; as consultants, 16; consultations for, 28, 35; evaluation of writing by, 71-72; intensive institutes for, 27-28; part-time, 28; productivity of, 35; research seminars for, 59; at research universities, 34-36; second-stage programs for, 13-20; support for, 28; writing workshops for, 17, 71-72. See also Teaching assistants
Faculty development: in community colleges, 22-23; need for, 94, 95; in secondary schools, 45, 46-47, 49-51
Fahrenbach, W., 17-18, 20
Faigley, L., 7, 12, 33, 40, 73
Fairfax County, consultants in, 50
Florida, writing mandated in community colleges of, 29
Flower, L., 48, 52
Flynn, E. A., 82, 87
Ford Foundation, 56
Forman, J., 82, 87
Foundations, funding by, 56
Freedman, S. W., 48, 52
Freshman composition courses, curricular change in, 6-7
Friedman, R. C., 32, 40
Fullerton College, linked courses at, 24
Fulwiler, T., 3n, 4, 5, 12, 14, 16, 18, 20, 27, 30, 61, 73, 74, 75, 82, 85, 86, 88
Funding: aspects of, 55-60; background on, 55-56; conclusion on, 60; continuous, 56-58; and redesign of program, 58-60

G

Garfield High School, achievement at, 48
Garies, R., 21n
Gazzam, V., 80-82, 88
General education committee, and curricular change, 7, 10, 97
George Mason University: Plan for Alternative General Education (PAGE) at, 7; upper-level writing course at, 101; workshops at, 15
Georgetown University, administration at, 63

U.S. Postal Service
STATEMENT OF OWNERSHIP, MANAGEMENT AND CIRCULATION
Required by 39 U.S.C. 3685

1A. Title of Publication	1B. PUBLICATION NO.	2. Date of Filing
New Directions for Teaching and Learning	0 0 1 - 8 0 1	10/26/88

3. Frequency of Issue	3A. No. of Issues Published Annually	3B. Annual Subscription Price
quarterly	4	$39 indiv./ $52 inst.

4. Complete Mailing Address of Known Office of Publication (Street, City, County, State and ZIP+4 Code) (Not printers)

350 Sansome Street, San Francisco, CA 94104

5. Complete Mailing Address of the Headquarters of General Business Offices of the Publisher (Not printer)

350 Sansome Street, San Francisco, CA 94104

6. Full Names and Complete Mailing Address of Publisher, Editor, and Managing Editor (This item MUST NOT be blank)

Publisher (Name and Complete Mailing Address)

Jossey-Bass Inc., Publishers, 350 Sansome Street, San Francisco, CA 94104

Editor (Name and Complete Mailing Address)

Robert E. Young, University of Wisconsin Center-Fox Valley, 1478 Midway Rd., Menasha, WI 54952

Managing Editor (Name and Complete Mailing Address)

Allen Jossey-Bass, Jossey-Bass Inc., Publishers
350 Sansome Street, San Francisco, CA 94104

7. Owner (If owned by a corporation, its name and address must be stated and also immediately thereunder the names and addresses of stockholders owning or holding 1 percent or more of total amount of stock. If not owned by a corporation, the names and addresses of the individual owners must be given. If owned by a partnership or other unincorporated firm, its name and address, as well as that of each individual must be given. If the publication is published by a nonprofit organization, its name and address must be stated.) (Item must be completed.)

Full Name	Complete Mailing Address
Jossey-Bass Inc., Publishers	350 Sansome Street San Francisco, CA 94104

for names and addresses of stockholders, see attached list

8. Known Bondholders, Mortgagees, and Other Security Holders Owning or Holding 1 Percent or More of Total Amount of Bonds, Mortgages or Other Securities (If there are none, so state)

Full Name	Complete Mailing Address
same as #7	

9. For Completion by Nonprofit Organizations Authorized To Mail at Special Rates (DMM Section 423.12 only) The purpose, function, and nonprofit status of this organization and the exempt status for Federal income tax purposes (Check one)

(1) ☐ Has Not Changed During Preceding 12 Months   (2) ☐ Has Changed During Preceding 12 Months   (If changed, publisher must submit explanation of change with this statement.)

10. Extent and Nature of Circulation (See instructions on reverse side)	Average No. Copies Each Issue During Preceding 12 Months	Actual No. Copies of Single Issue Published Nearest to Filing Date
A. Total No. Copies (Net Press Run)	1600	1663
B. Paid and/or Requested Circulation		
1. Sales through dealers and carriers, street vendors and counter sales	309	33
2. Mail Subscription (Paid and/or requested)	628	681
C. Total Paid and/or Requested Circulation (Sum of 10B1 and 10B2)	937	714
D. Free Distribution by Mail, Carrier or Other Means Samples, Complimentary, and Other Free Copies	129	214
E. Total Distribution (Sum of C and D)	1066	928
F. Copies Not Distributed		
1. Office use, left over, unaccounted, spoiled after printing	534	735
2. Return from News Agents		
G. TOTAL (Sum of E, F1 and 2—should equal net press run shown in A)	1600	1663

11. I certify that the statements made by me above are correct and complete

Signature and Title of Editor, Publisher, Business Manager, or Owner   [signature] Vice-President

PS Form 3526, Dec. 1987   (See instructions on reverse)